Stern Creek Road
A Murder Mystery

By

Tucker Walter

Up and coming author Tucker Walter has reworked her first novel into a spellbinding tale. She has weaved different angles of the same story together brilliantly. In the end, the story is just as dangerous as the curve on Stern Creek Road. – E. Throneberry.

A special thank you to my friends and family who have supported
and encouraged me.
My favorite Twin and Big Brother
J. Ruehle, E. Throneberry, and H. M. Horodeczny
And my final proofreader – Dad.

The guarantees of justice are only served when exacted
passionately, patiently, and personally.
- Ryann Kisne

Stern Creek Road
A Murder Mystery

Tucker Walter

Chapter 1

He parked his car toward the east end of the building. 18824 Whitfield Street, the lot of the Meijer Store, it was just as she described. The lights in the parking area were just beginning to come on, except the ones to the west near a sidewalk of trees, which were burned out. The plastic lamp covers were missing, and the posts were in dire need of paint.

She told him to park there, next to a broken-down silver four-door Dodge Neon. *Park in discrete and inconspicuous spaces, blend in,* he reminded himself. It sat in an apparent parking junkyard near two other vehicles missing windows and tires.

The Neon was sitting on four deflated tires; there were discarded plastics and papers surrounding it. Leaves, and small branches had fallen from the trees in recent months and were stuck to the windshield.

The lot held about 100 vehicles or so, and during the day, most of them filled with visitors from neighboring areas where the population didn't necessitate anything bigger than a gas station. His vehicle would undoubtedly appear as though it belonged. The older model light blue Ford Escort was an oddly painted color. It was mostly maroon with a white replacement fender and a dinged up rear bumper with bald tires; it would fit right in. *The space between would be an excellent spot to park*, he thought.

He was a moderately handsome young man, mid 30's or so, with a cute soft face. His brown hair cut short in the military fashion. *Girls are fascinated with the active army type; it makes them feel protected.* He was wearing slightly worn Tommy Jeans and a light green Hilfiger shirt that brought out his eyes. He was a little on the chubbier side; his love handles lapped his belt.

Self-esteem was not his strong point, but timeliness was. Jeremy glanced at his watch, 8:00 p.m. *I should run in and get her a little present.*

He recalled conversations during his secret club meetings; he had learned from professionals, and this was his third run. His mentors had purchased presents that would calm and comfort their 'dates.' It had worked the times before, and he convinced himself this time would be no different.

She said she lived a few blocks down Monica, so he figured he had some time to get in and out of the store without anyone noticing. He had about 25 minutes to spare if he was to be there at promptly 8:30 p. m.

He entered the store and kept his head down while he nervously glanced around from the left then to the right. He was anxious about his latest conversation with his "girl"- Sunblock13 and wondered if anyone could read his mind. He called her "Sunni." It was a name her grandmother had given her, and she allowed close friends and family to call her that.

He had been courting her on the Internet for months, and it had only been the last few weeks that he had gained enough of her trust to call her Sunni. She had promised him an evening alone, and he was looking forward to an evening of exploration. Today was the day he was finally going to meet her, and he did not want her to be disappointed.

He walked the aisles of teddy bears and stuffed animals and assortments trying to recall which animal she said she liked. *What did she tell me she wanted*? He was cursing himself for not remembering. *Try to bring a small gift that she will remember you by, but not overly apparent that she had not owned it before. She would not have the means to pay for it on her own;* again, the voice of his mentor rang in his head.

He wanted the gift to be something that reminded her of him. Maybe something she could take to school, or hide in her backpack.

He found a brown fluffy ballerina bear, one with a purple skirt and purple-laced ballerina shoes. *I think she likes dancing. Yes, she said dancing. This one is perfect. And purple, too,* he thought. He picked it up and walked to the register.

He walked to the checkout line and picked up a small bag of gummy bears and Hershey kisses. *I bet she'll like these, also. All the little girls seem to love these.* He spotted a gift bag covered in pink floating hearts while he waited and he thought it would be the perfect packaging and grabbed it up also.

"For your special someone?" The lady at the register asked. She was nice. She had been a cashier at the Meijer for several years, and thought she knew everyone in town; at least she acted as though she did.

"Yes, my little lady," he responded nervously. *She will be mine after tonight. My little lady.* He liked the sound of that and repeated it, smiling, "...they're for my little lady."

The bagger swooped up the items, "Do you just want them in the gift bag or do you want paper or plastic?"

Before he could answer the register lady started a barrage of questions, "You just passing through?" she inquired. Her voice was high pitched and whiny, "I've never seen you in here before." If there were ever a beauty parlor gossip club, she would be found at the center of it.

"How long are you staying in town? I know a nice little bed and breakfast north of town if you are interested?" She was more curious than helpful.

"Plastic. I'll do it myself," Jeremy's voice

deepened, and his annoyance became evident. He tried to remain calm, but the nosy cashier and bagger were paying so much attention to him that he became quickly irritated.

He grasped his change and receipt and jammed it into his right back pocket. He hurriedly picked up his items and the plastic bag, attempting to fill it on the way out the door. Damn plastic bag, I'm not handing her a damn plastic bag.

Disposing of it just outside the door, he carefully placed the ballerina bear, gummies, and kisses in the gift bag. *Very cute, I know she will love it.* He was proud of himself for his thoughtful idea.

He walked to the corner and turned down Monica Street with a quickened pace toward 51172. It was about 8:26 p.m. and the streetlights were seemingly lighting his path to her door. He believed it to be a sign of bright things ahead. His pace quickened, as he grew more and more excited, even skipping over a few cracks in the sidewalk. *Can never be too careful,* he thought.

First impressions are most important, and he wanted this to be the first of many visits. He stood in front of the little ranch house, brown with white trim and shutters, a large bay window facing the sidewalk with a small metal chain link fence around the property. The overhead garage door was open, and there weren't any cars inside.

That's my cue, no cars. His anxiety was waning as he glanced around; there were not any cars parked along the curb either, and the only vehicles he saw were lying cold and silent in neighboring driveways.

There were six other houses on this block. There was a bit of lawn between each home giving him the distance he desired. He had assessed they were at least double or triple lots, according to his online map survey of the area. *Always map the area so you can plan a 'run' route if needed.*

Each one had a fence of some sort, either chain link or private and this one was chain link. She had described these properties nearly perfectly, and he was beginning to trust his 'little lady.'

Jeremy stood at the edge of the sidewalk in the shadows for a few minutes watching the house. He made his final assessment that they would be alone, his confidence growing. He checked his watch for the fifth time; it was 8:30 p.m. exactly on time. He was always exactly on time.

Opening the fence gate to the front path he made sure it closed quietly behind him. He stepped across the grass section, feeling the moisture in the ground beneath his feet and hoped his shoes weren't getting wet. *If your shoes are wet, they may leave 'invisible' tracks in the house,* again the voice of his mentor.

Clutching his gift bag, he walked through the garage to the inside screen door. It was also open. *Don't knock, just come in. I don't want the dogs to bark.* He repeated Sunni's typed words as he pulled open the screen door and entered the home.

He stood near a washer and dryer and saw a small bathroom to the right. *Don't take off your shoes by the back door, in case someone comes home,* it was another memory of their previous online conversation, so he would leave his on despite what his mentor had suggested. His throat was instantly dry as he looked around to find her.

His heart was now racing, his concern rising as he continued down the entryway that led to the kitchen. The stove light was on, and a candle lit on the counter. The overhead garage door made a sluggish whiz-grinding sound as it began to close, which he barely noticed.

Oh, my God. Is this that stupid television show? Where is she? His nerves were rattled, "Hello..." a slight quiver in his voice. *Oh God, what am I getting myself into?* Visions of waiting cameras and uniformed police offers flooded his mind.

"Hello?" He asked again, his voice trembling. He advanced through the kitchen, setting the gift bag down on the table; he made his way cautiously into a living area. *This is a beautiful home. He noticed the curio cabinet with autographed baseballs of Lou Whittaker, Cal Ripkin Jr., and Pete Rose. Her dad is a sports fan, no doubt.*

Jeremy loved baseball; although he was never very good at it, the high school kids always made fun of him. They teased him incessantly for being a little too 'girly' for baseball.

A 65-inch flat screen television hung on the wall above the fireplace. The wood floors were polished to a shine, and he thought again of taking his shoes off, *your boots will leave shoe impressions on wood floors, invisible ones.*

"Jeremy?" A feminine voice called from behind him interrupting his thoughts.

A nervous ball of fire in his gut made him spin to the sound of her voice. "Yes, Sunni?" Jeremy blurted, wanting to say her name for so long out loud, "You, you, you are older than your profile lets on…" the stuttered words fell from his gaping mouth. He stood staring at her; she seemed to be in her late 20's, maybe 30, maybe his age. Even though he had planned for the probable Internet lie, he was still stunned.

Oh God, oh no, he placed his hand on the closest wall and tried to maintain his balance, a sphere of nerves found its way into his throat as he struggled for something to say. His hands were visibly shaking, and he was thankful he had set the gift bag down, lest he would have already dropped it.

"You were expecting 13? Really?" She said, barely above a whisper. She advanced his direction. If she was nervous, he couldn't tell. She was calm, collected and poised while she surveyed him.

"Can I get you a glass of wine? Perhaps a beer?" She genuinely offered. *It might take more than a beer to get him to relax,* she thought. She noticed his fists tighten up and kept her distance in case he decided to attack. She gently squeezed her necklace. It was a cleverly disguised alert device. Once if things were going well, twice for help. She was to give updates every fifteen minutes.

"Uhmm, I, uh I think I should go," he was looking for the television cameras, the police, and the guy from Dateline to appear and announce he had just been seduced by a police officer online pretending to be a thirteen-year-old girl. *You lured me. You tricked me into coming over with your seductive online conversations, promising sex and foreplay, your first time to be given to me,* his mind raced with defenses.

"I wasn't expecting..." his voice trailed off as he mustered up his strength and took one-step further away from her, but deeper into the living room. She was blocking his exit, and he didn't want to touch her, he was still paranoid that she was a cop and this was a setup.

"No, please, stay. Relax; you are not in any trouble. I'm not going to hurt you," motioning with her long arms and graceful hands, Sunni moved toward him but stopped well short. "See? There isn't anyone here but the two of us. Look for yourself."

He stood there, frozen; their eyes were locked. *What the fuck? Maybe I should sit. If I run out, there is probably a group of cameramen waiting for me. She isn't 13 after all, how much trouble can I get in?* Replaying his options, he decided that leaving was not one of them.

He decided he could not be arrested after she had trapped him, so what the hell, why not? After all, he had planned on an evening of fun, and she was not bad looking for a grown woman. *We've been chatting for months, how could I not see this? I've been so careful*, he thought. He could see the child in her as his eyes scanned her body.

She could see his hesitation, and at least he had not run through her to get to the door. She took a few steps into the kitchen and grabbed one glass and a bottle of white wine from the rack.

She is gorgeous, he thought. She was about 5'8", flowing brown hair, just below shoulder length, deep-sea blue glistening eyes. *She wants me,* he thought. He felt

11

his temperature rise, either from nervousness or excitement, he couldn't tell which. *She must have been hunting me online.* He cautiously watched her peel the label and seal from the bottle of wine. *Yes, she is seducing me.*

Walking back to him, she handed the bottle and the opener to him, "I have a terrible time trying to get these open without breaking a nail." Her bright smile was showing perfectly straight white teeth. Her hands to him seemed small, soft, and child-like.

He quickly uncorked the bottle and set the cork down on the end table. She held her glass out for him, expecting him to pour.

"Are you sure you don't want to share some with me?" She offered one last time.

"No, no, I don't drink," he lied. He needed to be sober. He cleared his throat carefully watching her move to the living area. She stopped at the couch and asked him to sit with her.

Waiting for his reply, she took a sip of her wine without taking her eyes from him. He watched her lips caress the edge of the glass. The liquid moistened her mouth, and he watched her tongue move along the rim with the expertise he had only witnessed on video.

"Come, sit," she patted the vacant seat next to her.

What the hell? What is this going to hurt? He thought and obediently sat down.

She reached to his leg and began circling his knee with her fingertips, "This is why you came here, isn't it, Jeremy?" Her voice was as seductive as the low cut dress she was wearing.

Sexy and chic, the little black dress had a halter neck and delicate rhinestone embellishment just below the bust. She wore a matching rhinestone watch and stone rings, one on each hand. The dress fell to a suggestive mini length, not quite reaching her knees. As she sat, he noticed her legs were shaved smooth, and he wondered if she had also shaved everything else.

He imagined her breasts would easily fit, if not be completely be covered by his hand. *Those are the right size for a woman,* he told himself.

Her waist was trim, and she seemed a bit athletic. Her arms were strong, thin and muscular.

"Do you want to talk first?" She asked, trying to make him more comfortable, "I must be honest with you. I'm not 13," giggling like a little girl. "I just wanted a nice young man to come to my house to take care of me. To treat me like a child," she began to explain, flashing those intensely beautiful blue eyes. "You seemed so sweet and sincere, and when you suggested we meet, I had to see you," she told him.

Feeling more relaxed now, he allowed himself to breathe a little deeper, "I thought this was going to be one of those television shows!" They both laughed, and she moved forward to touch his hair. He was cute, in a boyish kind of way with green eyes and a full face. He is shorter than I imagined, maybe 5'3". She noticed his jeans and matching shirt and that he took the time to clean his shoes, brown Dockers. *He dressed up for this,* she thought.

"How old are you?" She asked, leaning closer to him and sipping her glass of wine.

"Well, I'm 36. I'm so glad you're not the cops," he said nervously again.

Edging over, she moved her body closer to him, "Don't be silly, I'm just glad you came." She was close enough to smell him. *Is that women's cologne, in fact, isn't that what I said I liked*? She wondered.

"Come on now; you didn't think? But I do remember what you said, and I'm glad we had that conversation," she breathed a repeat conversation into his ear, one she had rehearsed over and over waiting for this moment.

"I will take care of you. I will be soft, and gentle, and make you feel like a woman. I must see you. I must hold you. I must have you wrapped in my arms." That was the first line he had used in their Internet conversation in an attempt to entice her.

His heart pounded at a quickened pace; the sweat beaded up on his forehead. *That's my line. She remembered my line, damn that really worked. That tactic has been brilliant.*

"You aren't exactly what I was expecting, and I'm not so sure I'm prepared, maybe I should leave," he was trying to be nonchalant, but just talking about sex with her was turning him on and he pressed his hand over the zipper of his jeans.

"Why don't we get more comfortable," she suggested. She gripped his knee harder with her right hand and gave a couple of tense squeezes. She pressed her right breast into his bicep, while she slipped off her shoes, "That it could be nice, it could be..." she was giving his written words volume. Her voice trailed off as she rubbed the inside of his thigh, skimming his growing, aching need with the backside of her hand. *That would hurt anyone 13 years old;* she thought as she pulled her hand back toward his knee.

He shifted and grabbed a couch pillow to cover himself, "Hey, what kind of dogs do you have?" Suddenly remembering she said she had animals. He had been there probably twenty minutes and hadn't seen nor heard any sort of animal.

"Don't change the subject!" She scolded him directly, regaining control of the conversation. Her voice stern and dark, but quickly turned playful as she tried to ease her nervousness, "Don't be shy, now, big boy." She toyed with her locket styled necklace pinching it between her fingers.

She needed him to stay focused on her. She set the wine glass down on the coffee table and turned on Sports Center to give them something else to talk about.

He was appreciative of the noise.

The first commercial aired, and she asked, "So, Jeremy, is it true, do you work as an account executive for APEX?" She was testing his Internet truthfulness. He claimed to be an account executive at one of the largest insurance companies in the nation; the headquarters was located in Waterford.

"Yeah, I landed that job two years..." stopping short, not wanting to reveal he had spent the previous five years in prison for a sex crime.

They spoke of his job for a few minutes, his big responsibility overseeing insurance fulfillments and supervising teams of representatives. She seemed crazy impressed, and he didn't mind 'courting' her with his status. Although she already knew his position as a claims settlement adjuster, she let him ramble.

He was the person that approved the claims based on field investigations. Her resources had already discovered his association with a fraud ring based on false or unscrupulous claims. He had accepted monetary bribes, and what could not be bought was traded.

Talking about himself made the arrogance radiate from his face. He was confident now that the police would not be involved, "Maybe I will take that beer now," half asking, half telling.

"There is a pool tournament on ESPN if you would like me to turn it on for you," she asked.

"Do you know how to play pool, or were you just saying that?" He asked her. His voice timid, but more firm. He was a pool enthusiast and wondered if she was lying about her interest as well. It was difficult to tell, he wasn't sure how many 13-year-old girls knew what the game was, but she did say her dad played, and her parents did have a pool table, and he saw now she was much older, so there was a chance.

She seized her opportunity, "Still don't trust me? Come on; I'll prove it to you. I will get you a cold beer out of the fridge, and if you want, the pool table is in the back room," she pointed the way.

She quickly got up and trotted across the kitchen to a foyer and disappeared from view.

She invited me here. She wanted me. She knew where this was going to lead. Jeremy rationalized that he would humor her with a game of pool, then lay her out across the table and have his way.

He stood up from the couch as best he could, pausing for a moment to let the blood rush from his pelvis, and walked through the kitchen.

He stepped into the back room and stared in amazement when he saw the regulation Olhausen Table. It was custom built with oak trim and velvet cloth reaching into every pocket, "Wow! You really do play!"

He was more excited now than before and momentarily distracted. He traced the table; it was solid, glazed with perfection. *Simply Amazing!* He thought. He circled the table and looked up. Jeremy would not get the chance to play.

WHACK! An earth-shattering thud, she throttled his neck with a thick wooden pool stick. She had wound up like a Louisville Slugger, took her best swing, and landed the perfect home run.

"Fuck you!" her eyes welled up with excitement. I did it! You fucking child molesting creep! I did it!

His limp body fell to the strategically placed carpet beneath him. His face crushed into the padding and he lost consciousness almost instantly. She watched as his body flopped and struggled for breath to no avail.

His trachea and larynx crushed inside his throat, a bloodless death of hands-free strangulation. She reassured herself that he was not getting up. His reflexes were instinctual and autonomic, and as he lay there convulsing, such as a fish out of the water - she was smiling inside.

Get your last breath asshole. She gave one squeeze of the necklace as she sipped her wine and waited for his pulse to cease.

Chapter 2

Waterford was a small city with a population of nearly twenty-five hundred. It was situated north of Havelock, North Carolina. It was the kind of city where the weather stayed seemingly beautiful, without much humidity.

There is one traffic signal on a cycled timer. The steady yellow was a little long, and the red too short, but nobody complained. The rest are yellow blinkers that occasionally required a full-fledged stop.

The old part of town still had cobblestone streets, and the tourist population was very low. There was a combined middle and high school, and even that shared a playground area with the Waterford Elementary.

The best place to eat was Amanda's Mexican Cuisine and the local cop hang out was Malone's down on Hamilton. The watering hole was Bob's where Thursdays drew the biggest crowd for karaoke.

The most exciting news in recent times was when the Meijer store bought an adjacent vacant lot and added 35 parking spaces.

There are two churches in town, a Catholic Church, and United Methodist, both of which were filled on Sunday's and Wednesdays. Tuesday nights the Waterford library hosts the middle school reading events, and on Saturdays, the bowling alley was filled with mixed leagues. The locals would find it difficult to use a word like 'busy' to describe any day in Waterford unless it was Monday night bingo at the American Legion.

The newly built Waterford Police Department (WPD) was a 12-hr station situated between the library and the middle school. The lobby doors are open from 8:00 a.m. until 8:00 p.m., if there was a need for an officer after 8 p.m., there was a yellow call box posted by the front door that was a direct dial to the county and state police dispatch center.

Until last year, the police department occupied an old three-room schoolhouse that the officers spent weekends off continually repairing the roof, floors, windows, and siding. The new structure was slightly larger than the Catholic Church, designed with main lobby security doors, which opened to the front desk.

The lobby waiting room held four chairs, and a small coffee table with current police bulletins stacked neatly along the edge. On one side of the desk was a hallway that leads to the chief's office, squad room, property, and equipment rooms. Another hall on the opposite side of the desk pointed to two locker rooms, male and female, which were divided by wall units for officer's road gear. The center of the building held a conference room, law library of sorts, and the detective bureau.   Shelves filled with motor vehicle codes, city ordinances, state and case laws divided three makeshift cubicles. Two small holding cells were nestled toward the sally port entry for secure prisoner processing and lock up. A small kitchenette allowed the officers a place to heat and store lunch.

An agency with nearly 14 employees, the Waterford Police Department had several beat cops, three detectives, one canine officer, the Captain and a number of civilian personnel who kept the records in order.

It was sex offender registration month and a busy time for the Waterford Police Department. Several months out of the year convicted sex offenders were required to register with their local police department. Records are kept and updated to include the offender's name and address changes, vehicle information, and emails and phone numbers.

Waterford had unusually large numbers of sex offenders visiting during these registry months. The laws had yet to require sex offenders to register in their own counties, and floods of strangers visited the police department to avoid notoriety within their own cities.

The ringing of the phone echoed at the desk, "Waterford Police, Officer Jones," he sighed heavily into the desk phone at the front lobby. Officer Randy Jones was relatively new on the force, but no stranger to police work. Jones' resume reflected a tour of police duty with the military. He was recently honorably discharged but speaks very little of his Internal Affairs assignment.

Rumors among the officers had him pegged for a sniper because he had completed special assignments alone abroad. He never confirmed or denied the rumor, but when he was on the range during qualifications, his shots never left the center circle, and he could shoot with his eyes closed, left or right handed. He was smart, ambitious, and angry and he was pissed he had to work the front desk during this time.

Officer David Cooper typically covered the first week of registration, leaving the second week for other officers to alternate. It was a tiring job, and Cooper seemed to have a better tolerance for the offenders, at least it seemed he had more patience.

This month Cooper was supposed to work the last week, but he extended his vacation by a week. Officer Reese, another beat cop, said he would work the second week to cover for him, but his son had broken his leg playing football, and he took a week off for the surgery and recovery.

Jones was thankful he only had to work the morning shift at the front desk handling the walk-in complaints, phones, and updating the sex offender registry.

"Yeah, uh...I need to register..." the male voice crackled and trailed off in a sheepish tone, barely audible. Ring. Ring. It was the last day of the month that sex offenders could verify their addresses without being arrested for violating their reporting duties.

"Do you mean the Sex Offender Registry?" Officer Jones asked abruptly. He was assigned to the county Sex Crimes Unit (SCU), and he had developed a complete disdain for sex offenders, especially pedophiles. The clientele made his blood boil.

He had forgotten there was a woman waiting in the lobby for traffic crash report that might have overheard him, but then again, Jones didn't care.

He was outwardly collected as he calmly stood up to straighten the mound of paperwork before him of the sex offenders that had so far failed to register, but the day was not over yet. Why do they wait until the last minute? Why can't they register in their own damn towns? He glanced at the list of names written on the indexed tabs, wondering if this is one of those creeps calling now with some lame excuse blaming someone else for their irresponsible behaviors. They were always the ones that tried to phone in and register- as if identity could be verified over the phone.

"Yeah, I'm supposed to, umm, come down and register," the voice said again, only a little more clearly.

He could tell this offender would rather not call, but his probation officer had probably threatened him with jail time and some fine if he didn't call by the end of the day. "Please hold sir," he answered two more calls before getting back to the sex offender inquiring about his registry date.

"Ok, so how may I help you, sir?" Jones said while motioning the last person waiting in the lobby to step forward. The sharply dressed woman handed him her business card with a traffic crash incident number scrawled across the back. He looked at the number and set the card down on the counter where she quickly swept it back into her purse.

Jones was listening for the caller to ask his question, "Hello, Officer Jones, may I help you?" He repeated as he turned to access the crash report files behind him.

"Ma'am, this is a crash from last year, it will be a few minutes for me to find it," he ignored the caller.

He was trying to accommodate everyone, but it only added more stress by answering the phone. He struggled to remain polite and tolerant although it had already been a long two hours for a man eager to be on the road "doing investigations" rather than 'secretarial' work at the desk.

Three more sex offenders entered the lobby and were anxiously waiting to sign the verification and update their information.

Thumbing through the crash reports Jones located the number on the card and absent-mindedly handed her the original.

"Oops. I need to make a copy of that," he placed the phone down forgetting he was still waiting for the caller to answer him back. I should just hang up on them, he thought and impulsively-he did.

He picked the report back up and jetted around the corner from the desk to make a copy. The phone rang yet another series of beeps indicating more than one call was coming in. He let it ring while he made the crash copy and returned the original to the file. He approached the woman at the counter with the copied report and answered the phone again before handing it to her.

"Waterford Police Department, is this an emergency?" Jones asked into the phone with his finger ready on the hold button. The caller blurted out a series of questions before he could tell him he would have to wait.

"I got to do that address thing. I got warrants," the young man stuttered, "I don't wanna get arrested. Are you guys gonna lock me up?"

Jones, irritated now with the caller, "Sir, you still have to register and update your address whether you have warrants or not. Bring your identification with you when you come in. We are open during the business day."

He took a deep breath and picked up the next ringing line, "Officer Jones," he was already spent.

A soft feminine voice on the other line had a few inquiries and began speaking right away, "Yes, ma'am, I'll try." He told her he would do his best to answer them.

"My name is Mrs. Elizabeth Hines, and I was wondering if my son had come down to register? He always signs up early, but he waited until the last minute this month. He is a sweet young boy, made a few mistakes you know, but I haven't seen him in a couple of days, and it isn't like him not to come home at night," she was rambling.

"He said he had a couple of meetings with his game team, I don't know where he hangs out and plays those video games, but that was yesterday, and I haven't seen him. You know, I keep telling him if he should quit playing those games and go get a job and a girlfriend..."

Jones suddenly realized he was still holding the crash report. Covering the phone mouthpiece, he mumbled, "Sorry ma'am. Here you go," he handed the waiting woman a copy of her requested report, and she quickly left.

"Ma'am, I don't know if he has registered or not. Does he live in Waterford? Our systems don't update immediately, so maybe he has and maybe he hasn't. It takes a little longer if he is from out of town," he snapped, he felt himself getting extremely short. His temper would periodically get the best of him, or maybe it was the PTSD. Either way, he had a very short fuse for sex offenders, and he recognized he was getting the end of his.

"What's his name? Okay, ma'am, please call back tomorrow. You will probably see him tonight. No, he isn't here in lock-up. Good day ma'am," he scratched the offender's name on a blank piece of paper and added it to the pile of non-compliant offenders.

"Thank you for holding, how may I help you?" Jones answered the last waiting line.

"Jarhead, you ready for lunch?" The familiar

sarcastically snide voice asked. Detective Mike Pierce, his partner in the SCU, was calling.

A fellow service member, Pierce affectionately called Jones 'Jarhead' out of respect. Pierce had not served in the heat of battle, but he had been assigned to a combat support hospital. The aftermath of the frontline terror strikes brought many victims to his mobile hospital tent. His voice was deep and unmistakable and it fit his build. He was structured to match, towering over his partner nearly 6 inches; Pierce stood about 6'2" with shoulders like a linebacker.

Jones had been so busy that he had forgotten about being hungry, "Yeah, but Jack's not back yet. He stopped in to say he was going to grab lunch before his shift, that was 45 minutes ago, he should be back any minute."

Jackson Delaney was the afternoon radio operator and dispatcher. He was due to be his replacement and Jones would have made him lunch if he thought Jack would have come in earlier to relieve him. The officers at the post called him "Jack" a nickname used affectionately by his brothers in blue.

The lobby clock bellowed the first of twelve strikes. Jack strolled in on the third stroke and picked up the ringing phone, "Waterford Police, Dispatcher Delaney." Placing his lunch on the counter, he waved his hand in a pushing motion for Jones to leave as he effortlessly picked up where Jones left off.

"Jack's back, I'll see you in a minute," Jones hung up and answered the next call, "Waterford Police, please hold." He placed the caller on hold, but before he could fill Jack in on the afternoon events, Jack was already deep into argumentative conversation with a subject on the phone. Having heard the excuses from sex offenders hundreds of times, Jack placed the phone down and stuffed his mouth with the remainder of his corned beef sandwich before listening to the end of the caller's rant.

"It's for you," Jones smiled at Jack, pointing at the phone. "Line two. Do you need anything else?" His voice trailed off in a half-hearted attempt to offer more assistance. He gathered two non-compliant offender sheets and jammed them into his absconder folder and promptly made his getaway.

He nearly sprinted from the front lobby toward the detective offices. He found Detective Pierce preoccupied snapping pictures with his new crime scene camera that he barely noticed him enter the room.

Pierce was obsessed with it. The department sent he and Jones to a mock crime scene seminar hosted by the State Police last month, and the cost of the training included a variety of crime scene equipment, including the camera.

Detective Pierce was an uptight kind of guy, yet easily excitable for a guy his size. Besides being an obsessive-compulsive germaphobe, he was extraordinarily egotistical and thought the spectacle of his physique was to make the ladies swoon.

Jones was surprised when Pierce submitted the request to spend money from the budget on something more than antiviral wipes and latex gloves. His assignment to SCU and residential verifications didn't help much with his OCD. However, he was a champion come time for inspection and audit.

"Ready to get some lunch?" Jones noticed he was hunched over his desk with the camera lens so close to it that he thought he was resting on it.

"Have you seen Terri? I thought she was coming in today?" Jones asked.

"Yeah, I'm ready. Did you know this new camera of mine takes such clear photographs one can easily read the year and mint location on this worn penny?" Pierce leaned up from the desk and sat back on his chair to admire the F-stops on the camera.

"Last month you didn't even know what an F-stop was, now suddenly you are an expert? And the camera is not yours," Jones reminded him.

"I thought I should get this warrant request done before I go. This guy we are looking for is a real asshole.

Both of the victims pointed him out in my photo line-up last night. I'm going to try to get it to the prosecutor tomorrow morning," Pierce picked up the criminal sex complaint he had been working.

"You said lunch," Jones told him.

Dismantling the telescoping lens, Pierce placed the camera in a Pelican Security box and slid it beneath his desk. Jones watched in amusement as he carefully picked up the coin.

"Terri went to that K9 seminar yesterday, remember? She isn't due back until tomorrow. I thought Reese was back today. Isn't he supposed to be working the desk? And I thought Cooper was supposed to be back, too. Where did he go this time?"

Pierce didn't wait for an answer as he proceeded to remove exactly one sheet of antiviral cleansing wipe and scrubbed both sides of the coin before putting it back into his pocket. He then swiped the desk left, flipped the sheet and swiped the desk right. Satisfied it was clean, he folded it in half, walked to the trash and gave it a toss before heading to the sink for his ceremonial scrub.

Jones believed his OCD and demand for cleanliness made him the perfect evidence technician. He was cautious not to contaminate any of the possible evidence, and his collection procedures were the best he had ever seen.

"No, not until tomorrow I guess. That prick, I'm sure he is somewhere with his 'Dragons.'" Anyway, before you get settled into your paperwork, did Jessica call me?" Jones asked.

Pierce looked at him with his typical fuzzy eyed look, "Oh, the 'Dragon Slayers' group. Seriously, a grown man and his interactive battle games with his new 'friends.' I keep telling him to get some real friends. Don't you think that recluse is withdrawn enough already?" His eyes rolled to the back of his head, "Jessica? You mean that chic the from FBI? The ex-agent?" His tone more of a statement than a question, "The one you are always raving about, yet no one has ever met her? Didn't you tell me she runs her own business now? What does she want with you, Jarhead?" Pierce joked.

"Yeah," Jones ignored the other questions and plopped down two folders marked "Absconder" on his desk.

"What's this?" Pierce asked. He opened one and reading from the center of the first page, it was marked in large print "CSC 1st- Kevin William Kramer, a white male aged 36, 5' 6" / 165 lbs. I take it this is the most recent upstanding, innocent, and condemned? One of the offenders who refuse to accept they must continue to register despite having served out their jail sentence? This guy too?" He looked at the second offender.

Pierce's questions were utterly sarcastic and rhetorical.

"These are our two Waterford guys that haven't verified their addresses yet. I made two file copies. And Jess, uh, Jessica asked me for a favor, so I told her I, uh, we would help if we could. She said she had been hired by a family to track down a possible suspect that they believed molested their daughter."

"Apparently, a family that can afford to have more than the police working on the complaint? Must be the trail is leading this way?" Pierce stated.

"To be honest, I do not have any information, except that the victim was around 4. The pay must be pretty good for Jess to take the case," Jones laughed, knowing Jessica did not do charity work.

"What in the hell is there to do in Waterford that so many of these guys end up here?" Pierce muttered half-ass hearing what he was saying.

Jones continued, "I'm hoping to meet up with her today and get the information on them so we can get started right away," he was eager to impress her.

Pierce placed the offender sheets back in the folder and put them on the corner of his desk; he decided to read through them after he had some food on his stomach and reached for the cola sitting on the table.

"You know what, I'm hungry, and this is warm.

C'mon, let's hit Malone's for lunch," he was already standing up to put on his jacket, and they headed for the door.

Jones stopped short and returned to the desk to grab the files. He put them in his briefcase, "You never know, maybe if I help her find her guy, she will help us find these guys, too."

Malone's was walking distance from the station and cops ate there with the 5-0 discount. A small, Irish pub open for lunch and drinks, next to Bob's bar it was the only other place in town serving alcohol before dinner.

"Hey, Tim!" Jones recognized his neighbor and gave a short wave as they walked in. Tim was propped up on the counter already enjoying his afternoon brandy. Tim was more of a fixture at Malone's than a customer, but seeing him there when the door opened made you feel at home.

Jones and Pierce sat in their usual spot near the side window with a good view of the parking lot. Like most cops, they never sat with their backs to the doors. If they had driven, they probably would have parked in front of the window, just in case anybody tried to mess with it.

"Finally, it's the end of the registration period for this quarter. Maybe we can go knock on a few doors tomorrow and flush these assholes out," Jones was excited to start the "track." To him, it felt like hunting, except he was in an official uniform and not buried along the landscape.

The waitress walked up to greet them as soon as Jones and Pierce sat down. Wearing blue jeans and a short sleeve Malone's t-shirt, Beverly pulled out her notepad, "Hi boys, will you guys be having the usual?"

"Coke, please. And the grilled chicken salad, Thanks, Bev," Jones ordered without looking at the menu.

"I'll have the same, it sounds good today," Pierce agreed.

She scratched down the order and grabbed up the menus. Damn, she looks good for 40. Pierce admired Bev's ass as she walked away.

Jones got back to business, "I want to round these guys up as soon as possible." He had reached into his bag and grabbed the file folder. He was trying to redirect the wandering eyes of his partner.

"Jarhead. You brought the fail file?" Pierce did not like to work while he was having lunch, much less bring documents and spread them across the table where bits of food and bacteria would infiltrate the paper for future infections.

The 'fail' files were the sex offender folders that contained names, all known addresses, and photographs of the offenders who were required to register and failed to do so. Most of the offenders in Waterford registered accordingly, but once a year the WPD submitted warrant requests to the county prosecutor for those who have failed to comply with the state ordered registry.

"Don't get ahead of yourself. We have to attempt to locate these guys first at their previously registered addresses," Pierce slipped into work mode.

"You are right, marine. We might need help finding these guys. I mean, you haven't done investigations on sex offenses since you thought the comic shop was selling porn magazines and videos, remember, Jarhead?" Pierce was half-chuckling. Last year Jones' nephew complained about one of his friends buying a 'porn' book at the comic shop. Pierce tried to laugh at the error of it, but he was seriously humiliated at the time.

Jones corrected him, "That was two years ago!" embarrassed at the memory. It had been his wild idea to do stakeouts and build enough evidence to get a search warrant for the raid.

He interrupted the teasing, "We only have these two guys who have failed to register, and I ran the list first thing this morning at the desk. Pierce, we only have these two offenders, so it shouldn't take us too long to find them. If they are still in Waterford, we WILL find them," his face grew stern and determined. Pierce nodded as he watched Bev walk back toward their table.

"Here you are," Bev set the drinks down and placed the straws on the table with napkins and silverware. She flashed her smile toward Pierce and spun around to the counter where the other patrons were eating.

After watching her walk away, Pierce questioned Jones, "You were saying at the office...Jessica?"

Jones began, "Yeah, she is doing some hunting also. I figured we could use her help to get a head start on locating..."

Pierce cut him off again– "You know she isn't your type, yet you keep calling her. Figure it out Jarhead – she doesn't want to date you."

"Yeah, well she called me this time. Didn't you hear anything I said? She wanted to talk about someone that might be in Waterford. The new case I was telling you about," he was interrupted when Pierce's phone rang.

"Hey, Terri," Pierce answered, "What's up?"

"Hi Mike, did you see the schedule?" Terri asked. Terri Bradford was one of the lead detectives with the most experience and training at the Waterford Police Department. She was also the only one allowed to call Pierce by his first name.

Terri was the smallest, and maybe the tallest, police officer of the group. She was a full 2 inches taller than Pierce and towered over Jones.

Her slender athletic build made her waist look very small when she strapped on her gun belt. She was also the department's K-9 handler and could outrun any one of the area officers for miles. She kept her soft brown hair cut short and didn't wear much jewelry. Her wrist was adorned with a large faced watch that covered an infinity tattoo she had gotten at the beginning of her longest relationship.

She was unbiased and open-minded. She had dated a couple of men and was known to date a woman or two. She had a reputation for getting what she wanted, with little regard for the partnership. She had been single for several years, and she had no intentions of settling down.

Jones' phone rang as well. He excused himself from the table to answer it while Pierce talked to Terri.

"I haven't looked, but I can give you a call when I get back to the station," Pierce replied about the schedule.

"I requested tomorrow off, and Cap said he would have it on the posted schedule by today," Terri told him.

"I could shoot you a text later if it's up and let you know, but I would assume you are off," Pierce was inspecting his silverware as he spoke. Satisfied that he had adequately sanitized them, he began wiping the front of his glass with a napkin as he asked Terri if she would join them for lunch.

"We are at Malone's if you are in the neighborhood," he suggested she could stop by to meet them.

"Nah, I'm running errands, besides I have to drop Duke off and I have to go for a run yet and get a shower. I'll catch up with you guys later," Terri explained. "By the way, are you guys going to make it out to Eddie's party? I told Trish we would all be going."

Pierce thought for a moment, "So he did get that scholarship to Central N.C.?"

"Yeah, pretty sweet, huh? So, ok, you guys are going to be there, right?" Terri was almost ordering him.

"I'll talk to Jones and tell him he is going. I'm sure we will both be there. You can count on us ma'am," he playfully acknowledged her senior rank.

"Where is he? I thought he was with you?" Terri asked.

"Jones went outside to take a call. His old girlfriend called him wanting some information," Pierce explained.

"Jessica? The one he has been after for years?" Terri was familiar with his infatuation for her.
"That's the one. Jessica is cute though. We will see you tonight. Maybe he will bring her too," Pierce told her then set the phone down and began to eat.

Jones returned to the table and sat down, "She's on her way into the restaurant now. She said she was parking, ah, there she is now."

Pierce looked over his Coke to watch her walk in. He stood and waited for her to sit. I need to get out more. Pierce thought to himself as he admired her breasts.

Randy Jones and Jessica Patterson were old high school friends; in fact, they dated through their junior year. They were separated just in time for Jessica to take a girlfriend to senior prom.

After school, they both pursued careers in law enforcement, Jones enlisted with the Marines, then attended a local police academy.

Patterson found her way through the ranks of the Federal Bureau of Investigations. She accepted a duty disability retirement after a severe crash left her "disabled" according to FBI standards. She still had many FBI resources and had started her own private investigations business and was doing quite well.

"Thank you. Jessica Patterson. Nice to meet you," she extended her hand to Pierce.

Pierce's eyes were affixed to her, "My pleasure." He had just cleaned his glass, silverware, and hands again.

"Thanks for meeting with me, Randy," her eyes were bright as she continued, "I was hoping you could help. I've tracked a guy to the Waterford area but have come up empty. Since both of you know everyone in town, it may be easier for you to point me in the right direction."

"Randy told me the two of you are heading up the SCU, and I think any information you can give me about where they might be hanging out, at least locally, might help me find this guy," she explained to Pierce.

Jones motioned for Bev to bring Jessica a cup of coffee and she was over within a minute. She had been watching the table, curious about this 'stranger' in her diner.

"My client has political ties and has been trying to

help his constituents fulfill a couple of promises. There had been a push for a new initiative with the sex offender registry. He has targeted the smaller more rural areas of the state, and his friends are taking a firm stance against criminal offenders-he is hoping it will help them reach a larger voter base. Unfortunately, my client's daughter fell victim to a predator and that predator was never held accountable. His daughter was so smitten with her new 'lover' she refused to cooperate at all with the investigation or prosecution," Jessica paused to take a sip of her coffee, she was very matter-of-fact.

"Cream or sugar?" Pierce had barely heard a word she said, his gaze still fixated.

"So your client wants to seek a little justice for his daughter? You can't retry a case, or force a victim to testify you know," Jones was paying careful attention.

"My client believes the grandchild is in imminent danger and wants him tracked down for a welfare check. Maybe a little surveillance," she explained.

"What makes you think he would be hiding out in Waterford?" Jones asked.

Pierce piped in, "I'm sure she knows what she's doing, Randy."

Don't be a douche; Jones muttered to himself, "I didn't know business was going so well...who is this client of yours, huh? Is this guy on the sex offender registry?" Jones was hopeful he could help.

Jessica didn't have time to answer before Jones started speaking again.

"I'm sure you know the registry, and we use the public registry as a valuable resource for tracking these guys down. We are running the specialty unit in our department, but we are focused on primarily those non-complainant offenders that have served their sentences, presently on probation, or reporting probation for committing a criminal sexual offense. They have a past conviction for criminal sexual conduct (CSC), any offense involving sexually deviant behavior, have displayed sexually deviant behavior in the commission of any felony offense, or have admitted to committing sexually deviant behavior. Our main purpose is to make sure they verify," he hardly took a breath in his explanation.

"Randy, you know I'm impressed already. I'm very proud of you," her eyes smiled at him.

He blushed and said, "Some sex offenders require a higher degree of supervision than other offenders. We don't have but a few on probation that live in our area, but I can call over to the County and ask around, I just need the names."

Bev had returned to the table to take Jessica's order.

"I'll just have the coffee, thanks, I already ate," she was polite.

"We would be honored to help any way that we could," Jones reiterated, he was ready for a little more excitement.

Pierce was still watching Jessica, zoned in on the shapeliness of her body as he finished his grilled chicken. He signaled to Bev for a refill without taking his eyes from her.

"We have our offenders in check!" Jones boasted. He was very proud of his accomplishments.

"The SCU has managed to get excellent information on our offenders, even information on the people they tend to associate with," he tried again to impress her with big words and complete sentences, the kind he could not put together when they dated.

"Wow. It sounds like you have finally gotten your act together," Jessica looked at him softly, watching him speak. She tried to appear interested.

"You said you had a couple of guys you couldn't find this go-around. How will I be able to help you?" Jessica referred to her vast experiences and contacts within her old department. She was the agent assigned to the area that included Waterford.

Pierce jumped in, "We have ten child molesters in our city." His aggravation and disgust was unmistakable.

"All of them register, and register on time. At

least they have all registered on time since I've been here. And the ones that don't, we knock on doors and find them. We obviously can't check their addresses outside of Waterford, but we have a couple who haven't verified their addresses that still report that they live here," Jones explained the problem.

"We may need help locating these guys," Jones asked of Jessica without forming the question.

"You can get us access to personnel records, tax records, lien holder agreements, virtually every database that would enable us to locate these sick bastards."

Pierce cut in, finally ready to blink, "We would do it ourselves, but last year with budget cuts, the department had to stop shelling out funds for special IT programs we weren't using. We are lucky to have LEIN (Law Enforcement Information Network) still, so we can run driver's licenses and warrant checks," his voice thick with sarcasm.

Looking at Jones, Jessica expected him to be prepared, "Do you have their names and some background for me to review?"

He nodded, "Yes. I have completed everything, and I have it ready for you. All of their personal information, last known addresses, and places of employment. I know it is only two, but it seems they have dropped off the face of the Earth. And we don't want this to get out of hand."

He was a little embarrassed about making such a huge ordeal out of the matter, but he was the type of man who hated loose ends. "I know it doesn't seem like much to an ex-agent and busy business diva, but if you could find the time to help us track these guys down, you know since you are going to be in Waterford."

Jones already had his 'absconder' folders on the table, "We were just about to discuss these, but you can have this folder. I already made copies for us." He slid them across the table.

"These are Waterford's sex offenders who have missed the registration deadline, I know there are only two, and I scratched down a third name, but I'm not sure if he has verified or not. So two for now, but two nonetheless."

Jessica didn't bother to look through the folder; instead, she placed them in her attaché case and stood to leave, "I will see what I can dig up. Are you available tomorrow, Randy? Maybe I can bring my file to you?" She avoided eye contact with Pierce; she could still feel his eyes burning her chest.

"Of course, Jess. Call me at home later and we can discuss a time," he smiled.

"Great! I'll contact you tomorrow – and maybe I will have some information on your cases by then as well," she smiled as she dropped three bucks on the table for the coffee and headed for the door.

Pierce stood up as well; he just couldn't let her leave without another look at her rear-end.

Chapter 3

"Where have you been all night?" Ryann tried to keep her voice low as Terri stumbled through the door with Trisha in tow; both of them emitted the unmistakable pungent odor of barroom smoke, liquor, and breath mints. She had been standing at the sink washing her glass when she saw the car roll into the driveway.

Terri had been dating Ryann Kisne a short time, and when they first met, she fell instantly infatuated with her deep blue eyes and straight brown hair. There was something about her penetrating soft look that had roped her in. She just couldn't shake the feeling that she had seen her somewhere before, that maybe she had known her somehow, but knew she had never met her.

"You know where I've been," Terri's voice was rough and hoarse from the late hour and crowded bar. "I told you I would be home in the morning; it's just later than I thought, err ah, earlier!" She turned and laughed at Trisha who still had bits of paper in her hair from the streamers and pop caps.

"I'll say, it's already 330!" She took the car keys and their jackets as she walked by them to let Duke outside, "Your boy has been waiting for you since you left this afternoon."

Ryann explained how Duke had been patiently laying by the door and hypersensitive to every sound.

"Duke!" Trisha stopped him before he could get outside. She waited for him to sit obediently while she reached out to pat his head. Despite her inebriation, she knew a police canine was not an animal that should be startled or touched unexpectedly, but she felt secure since she treated him like he was her own.

Trisha Medley and Terri Bradford had been friends for years, and Duke was very familiar with her, yet she did not take chances. Trisha worked as a waitress at Bob's bar, she knew everyone in town, and she had a knack for encouraging everyone to close the place down with her. Her infectious laughter, gritty sense of humor and colorful language only added to her allure.

Tonight was a special evening though; her son Eddie graduated and had just accepted a major university football scholarship, and it seemed the whole town was celebrating.

"Oh babe, I wish you were there, Trish had Eddie, Randy, Mike, and Mark rolling on the floor!" She tried to describe how the regulars responded to Trisha's antics, but it was difficult to understand what she was saying between the bouts of laughter.

"I can't wait to hear all about it, but after you change for bed, now go. I'll let Duke back in."

Terri was already walking down the hall toward the bedroom while Trisha headed to the bathroom. Several minutes later Trisha emerged and headed straight for the living room. She tripped on the edge of the rug that padded her walk across the hardwood floor. Stepping by Duke didn't help much either; trying to avoid an excited German shepherd pup is like swimming without getting your hair wet.

Trisha fell face first on the couch and pulled the knitted blanket from the top edge, "Good night you two-don't keep me up all morning," and was at once asleep.

Terri made her way to the kitchen to get a drink of water and grabbed some Motrin while Ryann popped in two pieces of bread in the toaster.

"You should eat something; it will make you feel better when you wake up. Don't you know you have to work today? Every time you go out with her you come home drunk," she sounded put off.

Terri didn't answer.

"As I remember you have to be at work early today, don't you? Isn't there an important meeting with the other detectives, SCU, right?" Ryann was extraordinarily patient and level headed, and she had a memory that didn't lapse.

Terri thought she could be a little intrusive for a

37

person she had only been dating a short time, "How come you always know my schedule? Sometimes, better than I do."

When they first started talking Terri thought it was cute and attractive how much Ryann wanted to know about her work. She was always asking about her co-workers, the office, and investigations. Terri even talked to her about the toughest and most interesting cases, and she had helped her solve who-done-it embezzlement from the Dollar Store.

Ryann seemed to not only to be curious but almost infatuated with the particulars of crime scenes. This week Ryann had been irritating her with so many questions. She seemed to have details that Terri didn't remember sharing with her, but she chalked it up to her ability to draw excellent conclusions with limited information.

"Eat, please. It will help you sleep, and you need something in your stomach with the meds," Ryann set the plate down in front of her.

Accepting the buttered toast, she snapped, "Seriously, Ryann? I'm not drunk. You should have met us. Why don't you want to meet my friends and co-workers anyway? And when have I ever been late for work?"

"Stop Terri. I guess I was expecting you home sooner. I'm kind of tired also and I have a morning consultation, too. You know I have deadlines. I just wanted to feel more prepared. I'm sorry."

"C-MET clients?" Terri asked, referring to her online business. She told Terri it was a private consulting firm with a client list from around the country. It seemed some days she was tied to her laptop, continually responding to client needs. Terri didn't pay attention when she tried to explain what the acronym stood for or what the company was about, she was more interested in Ryann's looks than anything else.

Ryann turned the focus back to Terri, "Looks like you had a perfect time without me. I bet David will be sorry he missed this one," she commented aloud.

"David? That boob. He isn't back from vacation. I thought I told you already? I could honestly care less if he comes back to work. He is such an anchor. He has been so preoccupied with his gamer group; in fact, the group has consumed him. He's worse than a kid with a new PlayStation," she rinsed her hands in the sink and dried them with a paper towel.

Ryann wrapped her arms around Terri's waist and walked her to the bedroom, "Come on, you need some sleep."

Terri leaned on her heavily as they waltzed to the bedroom together, slowly. She was much taller than Ryann, and when she put her head down on her shoulder for help to sit on the bed, she nearly pushed her over.

Ryann had spent the last two months building her trust, and finally, the weight of her body was evidence that Terri was letting down her wall of protection. She took slow deep breaths as she laid her back to unbuckle her belt and slide off her jeans, "I love these jeans on you, they make you look so thin, they are a perfect fit," Ryann whispered.

"You do?" Terri spoke clear and soft, her eyes closed.

She recognized the tone in her whisper as Terri began to reach up to her. "Mmm...your skin is so soft," she said, her hands moving swiftly to remove the blouse Ryann was wearing.

Suddenly, in one sure movement, she leaned up to pull Ryann onto the bed with her. Unable to keep her balance, she collapsed over her as they fell back, their noses touching. Firm and deliberate Terri encased her mouth around Ryann's and between breaths she whispered, "Shhhh, be quiet," her words echoed into the back of her throat.

Ryann tried to wriggle Terri's shirt off knowing there would not be much time before she would be unable to remove it. The shirt was pinned between them as she struggled to edge it passed her lower set of ribs.

Without hesitation, Terri swept it off and rolled Ryann to her back. She pressed her body into her and Ryann felt her breasts supple and formed.

Terri's mouth moved downward across Ryann's face stopping to kiss the soft spot between her neck and shoulder. As if she had just woken from a long nap, she effortlessly washed her hands down her biceps, across her elbows and pinned Ryann's wrists to her side.

Sensing her strength was powered by craving and sheer will, she tried to lie back, but the heightening anguish of desire (and partially knowing how she made her body react to her touch) made it impossible not to squirm.

"Terri, I ..." Ryann's words trailed off as she felt the heat, the spark that was kindling toward flames, her hips pressing harder into her.

"Shhhhh," Terri reminded her again of the fixture on the couch, "No need for words, love. I have plenty of time to sleep."

Ryann decided resistance would be futile. Once Terri felt her body give in, she released her hands and their mouths embraced, warm, soft. She moved her hands along Terri's side to her back. She rubbed gently before digging her nails into her skin and began scratching down the center. She knew Terri was already tired, and this would be just what she needed to fall asleep.

It wasn't ten minutes before Terri was snoring. She squeezed from beneath her and left her lay in a heap. Covering her with the sheet and comforter, Ryann kissed her goodnight.

Before she left, she set the alarm clock and left a note on the kitchen table that read: *I left early to finish some work. Have a wonderful day and text me when you get a chance. Hope to see you this evening*- Ryann

Chapter 4

"Sir, today is the 16th, how come you missed the registration period?" Officer Jones asked in his usual 'you disgust me' tone. He was talking to the Caucasian male that had walked into the lobby at 8:01 a.m. He was there to verify his address and had already missed the deadline.

"I forgot," he lied. He shifted from one foot to the other and looked irritated that he even had to register. He pushed his identification card through the glass window for Jones.

"51172 Monica Street, Waterford. Is this your correct address, sir?" He was not in the mood for this guy. He recognized his name from the short list he compiled yesterday of late reporting offenders.

Numerous anonymous tips had been flowing into the 'Report a Creep' line advising that this guy had been living at an unverified address.

"George Edward Moore, living in the City of Waterford, 51172 Monica Street, criminal sexual conduct in the 1st degree. Is that correct, sir?" He asked out loud, knowing that he has outed his secret with a lobby occupied by two individuals filling out bicycle registration applications.

They both looked up wishing they had taken their applications home to complete the paperwork. Instantly the eldest, and most likely the older sister, grabbed the other's hand and moved them to the farthest seating point of the lobby to protect themselves from the convicted child molester.

"Yes," the sex offender said beneath his breath. "You are an asshole you know that? Where is the other cop that registers us? You listen here; I paid my price and did my time. You don't have to treat me like dirt in front of these people," he was humiliated.

Jones kept about his business pulling up Moore's information on the sex offender database, "It seems we completed a residence check at this property nearly two weeks ago, and the property was vacant. You don't live there, sir. Where do you live?" Jones read the investigative notes and then shifted his eyes to Moore, "Well?"

"No, it is not vacant," Moore argued. He insisted that he still lived on Monica Street. Knowing that failing to change his address and reporting that change to the registry was a felony and could land him right back in prison, but he had been registering at this address for several months without question.

"No, sir, it is a vacant property. If I register you at this address, I will also cite you for reporting a false address and failing to report within the required reporting period." Jones knew there were a few homes for sale on the block from his patrol beat, but he was not sure if this was one of them.

A citizen tip indicated the property was listed for sale for the last several months.

"What? I came in to register, and you need to register me. This is bullshit! That other cop never questioned my shit. I said I lived there and I do," Moore was upset but rather calm. He gathered his driver's license and stood facing Jones.

"This is bullshit!" He repeated, "You can come to my house anytime, I'm not always there, but that is my address! Are you going to register me or not?"

"Sir, if you raise your voice or use profanity one more time in my lobby, I will arrest you for disorderly conduct! Now, keep it down," Jones informed him, staring him directly in the eyes. His blood pressure was rising at the site of this man.

"I do live at 51172 Monica Street," he was still pleading his case and trying to avoid a potential citation.

"Sir, take your things and this change of address form. I'm going to register you at your Monica Street address, but rest assured, one of our officers will be at the address today to see that you are telling the truth," Jones decided it was better to at least have an address on file for the offender than nothing at all.

"We are open until five tonight. I expect you will be back before then with an updated address, sir. I will verify you at your correct address then, sir." *You lying piece of shit,* he thought. Jones informed him as he handed back his identification.

"Fucking prick...you guys are all assholes," Moore maliciously remarked under his breath as he quickly headed for the exit.

Jones looked at his watch, *shit, 8:10, where is Jack, and I'm going to be late,* he thought. Just then Jack walked in the door, he had bagels and coffee for the crew. Jones decided he could be forgiven.

"Plain bagels, cream cheese, and hot coffee. Cooper asked me to stop and get some on the way. He said he was going to do it, but he is running late for the meeting. Said he got in late last night. I'm going to put these back in the kitchen; I'll be right back," Jack scurried down the hall.

"All good, Jack," Jones took a moment to gather the files he had been running for the meeting and was prioritizing the Monica Street address when the phone rang.

"Waterford Police, Officer Jones," he was stern but polite.

"Officer Jones, this is dispatch. We have a third party caller who says her son found a shoe and a jacket along Stern Creek Road. The caller says he was looking around for the other one and noticed what might be a person laying in a field. It didn't look like they were breathing," the dispatcher sounded rattled.

Jones was instantly excited, "What? Where? Is the caller still on the phone? Tell them not to touch anything – we will be right out. What's the cross for Stern Creek?" Jones was jotting down details and directions.

"Do you want me to page out K-9?" Dispatch

asked.

"I will get her on the phone, and I'll call out Pierce," Jones was anxious to make the calls himself.

The distant sound of cymbals clashing rang out from her rear pocket. Terri grabbed her cell phone and answered quickly.

"Terri?" The voice on the other end, "It's about time you answered your damn phone," the voice was notably harsh.

"It's Jones. Can you start for Stern Creek Road with Duke? Someone called dispatch and said there might be a body lying out there. I'm headed out there with Pierce. I'm just waiting for him to get his camera stuff together. I think it's near Highway 612," his speech was quickened, and Terri barely comprehended what he had said.

"I'm already on my way in for that meeting Randy. Did David come in today? He was supposed to be back. He was going to do the elementary school safety presentation for me so we could discuss tracking down these sex offenders as soon as possible..."

"Terri, listen. Don't come here – we are going to Stern Creek Road, did you hear what I said?" Jones was more persistent.

Terri remained silent for a moment, replaying the conversation she filtered out her mental preoccupation with the meeting, "Wait, what? Did you just say a body? Like a human body? What makes you think it is a body? Be serious Randy – I said I was on my way in."

Terri's questioning became more directed, but she still thought he was teasing her. They were always talking about working a big case together, but Waterford was such a sleepy town they were thankful nothing too serious had ever really happened.

"No, no, I am not kidding. Dispatch just called, and I told Pierce. Cooper isn't back yet. We are leaving in a few minutes. How long will it take you to get out there?" He asked.

"It'll take us about 20 minutes to get there from here, can you make sure the scene is secure and make sure we have a good perimeter set with the crime scene tape and keep the radio traffic to a minimum?" Terri instructed, recalling how about six months ago one of the county deputies had given his girlfriend his other radio.

She was a news reporter for the local paper and had written a piece on a full-scale murder investigation before even arriving on the scene. The entire county was in an uproar over a dead deer on Route 3.

Jones assured her he would get started on it as soon as they were on scene and hung up. His previous training had taught him in times of high anxiety to take deep breaths, collect his thoughts, 'center yourself' they had said.

He had a "go kit" already prepared – briefcase with consent forms, graphing paper for mapping crime scenes, evidence tags, and the like. Pierce was way ahead of him though; he had been the evidence technician for Waterford nearly his entire career. His items were in utility boxes and a gear bag. They loaded the equipment and themselves into the same patrol vehicle and headed to the scene.

"You ready, Duke? We have another job to do fella, you ready?" She nervously asked him, as if he could respond. *This might just be something. A box, shoes on the road, maybe a hit and run that knocked the poor victim right out of his shoes? Maybe bloody clothes and a smoking gun, too. There hasn't been but two non-natural deaths in Waterford County in the last seven years. And we have never had a homicide,* Terri thought.

Pierce insisted on driving. His slow pace aggravated Jones. He was beginning to withdraw emotionally and by the time they pulled down Stern Creek Road he was stone cold quiet. There was a young man standing near a shoe on the shoulder; he was waving to them.

Pierce slowed near the boy and turned to Jones, but before he could say a word, he saw that he was already stoic and fiercely focused on the boy. Jones was out of the patrol vehicle before it had come to a complete stop.

"Are you the 911 caller?" His voice was deep and sure.

The young man, about 12 years old was standing next to his bicycle. "Yes, I was riding my bike to school, and I saw this shoe," he pointed toward the front tire. There was one light brown work style lace up boot. The boot was untied and on its side.

Maybe a man's size eight Jones guessed, "Ok. Then what?"

"I stopped and looked at it. I picked it up at first, but then I saw that green shirt and that big cardboard box," the boy pointed to the shirt in the grass and about 20 feet out, a cardboard box.

"I was going to check it out, but then I saw those jeans coming out of the box, and it looked, well, like a leg. So I stopped and called my mom at work. She said to stay here and wait for you guys 'cuz she was going to call."

Jones took out his notepad and began to write when his phone rang.

"Officer Jones," he already knew it was Terri.

"Randy, you guys there yet? Is it a body? Duke and I are on the way, should be there in about 15 minutes or less."

"I am out here now, and it does look pretty suspicious, I mean with that size box laying in the field," Jones stared at the box as he spoke.

"How big is the box? You don't think it is possible for a box to be in a field?" Terri asked.

"It's possible because I am looking at it. I haven't walked up to it yet. Terri, there is this boot and a shirt lying here, too. And I'm still waiting for slow ass Pierce to get out of the damn car. He is busy organizing his folder for some investigative notes. I swear his OCD kills me sometimes," Jones was bordering on severe irritation.

"I mean, I, uh, the boot has a couple of smudges on it, grease or blood, or something. I started to walk up to it but stopped when I saw what looked like jeans coming from the box itself, and most likely attached to a leg. Yes, I can almost make it out from here," Jones told her.

He weighed the avenues of the potential ensuing investigation, "I thought you and Duke might want to come out before I got closer. I know how you don't like when people mess up the dog track before you have a chance to run him over it."

"Yeah, we are almost there. I'm turning off highway 612 now, should be another ten minutes," Terri said, a hint of excitement echoing in her tone. *At least it is daylight and not midnight this time, it's beautiful, the sun is coming up, and that will help us see more clearly.*

She reminded herself of crime scene protocol, *don't forget photographs, crime scene log, witnesses, and interviews. Maybe if it is really blood, I can get the accident Reconstructionist from the Highway Patrol to come out with his laser to measure the scene.* They had an excellent computer program to develop realistically generated crime scenes. Terri tried to stay focused on the probability that an injured animal crawled into the box and died, but she had this nagging feeling something was wrong.

"And Randy, give Mike a break. He is incredibly meticulous, and despite being a pain in the ass most of the time, he is excellent at gathering and documenting forensic evidence."

"Terri, I know – just get here," he turned back toward the patrol unit and gave Pierce the stare down.

She hung up, and the phone rang right back. *This better not be Randy telling me about a dead raccoon,* Terri thought as she answered the phone.

"Hello, this is Terri," she said as professionally as possible, thinking there was a chance it could be her Captain calling to figure out just what the hell was going on.

"Hello, this is Terri," she repeated into the phone. No answer. There wasn't a dial tone either and checking the cell phone face; the time was running.

"Hello," Terri said, slightly irritated. She jammed her finger on the off button then quickly hit the incoming call list. Unknown caller. Second time today. Maybe it's a telemarketer. Probably got my number from one of those Internet lists. Terri dismissed the call as she turned down Stern Creek Road.

Terri pulled up leaving Duke in the truck with the window down. She wasn't sure she would need him and went to make an assessment first. Pierce was standing over his opened camera case, which he had placed on his patrol car hood.

"Hi, Mike. Randy, what did you guys find?" Randy was already in her face explaining, "Seems we've got a box with a shoe near it, the shoe might have some blood on it. Couldn't really tell if it was blood or water, but either way, we didn't get close enough to it. The Johnson boy found it while riding his bike to school. And we left it alone Terri. We didn't even walk any closer than this. We really couldn't see inside, it looks like it may be laying on its side, and then you showed up," he talked excitedly fast.

"What is that laying in the grass? There, are about ten feet up? Did you walk around it?" Terri pointed to something brown and fluffy.

"Looks like an animal, I hadn't noticed it, a squirrel maybe," he guessed.

"We didn't want to walk around your scene, so we've been patiently waiting."

Pierce glared at Randy, "Well, waiting, anyway."

"Mike, did you already take photographs? Black and white and color film?" Terri questioned, hoping he had already done so.

"No, Terri it's been like ten minutes. But I will get started as soon as you guys figure out if it is a possum or not." Pierce believed they were getting excited about nothing.

"Alright, anything else I should know?" Terri asked, hoping there wouldn't be anything more to this dead raccoon scenario. Terri was sure the two of them would have checked out the box by now, but she was thankful they had waited.

"Well, let's walk up and check it out, Randy. See what we have, maybe it's a donation box dumped from the back of a Salvation Army truck." Terri stopped before inspecting the first shoe on the shoulder.

"Young, man, could you take your bike and wait over there by that tree please?" She pointed the boy out of the way to stand by a large tree across the road. She didn't want him to see anything if there was anything to see.

"Mike, Randy and I are going to walk straight out to the box and see if those clothes are your size," Terri smiled and started along a straight line directly to the box. It was about 25-30 feet out from the road, and it appeared to have been dumped recently.

There were grass stains on the side of the box that she could see and it was moderately crushed-or pushed over. It looked like someone had to drag it to the field and left it. The grass was tamped down already where they started to walk.

The first item in the grass was the boot. From the boot, they made their way toward the shirt, "Yep, light green shirt, and this is a brown stuffed animal."

"It is looking more and more like a donation box, Terri," Jones seemed incredibly disappointed, but even he knew that casual clothes, shoes, and household items could easily be donated items.

"Let's approach from the other side," she suggested so we don't screw up a potential track. A glass bottle of Coca-Cola lay covered in the grass. The weeds had grown up, around, and over it, so it could not be part of the crime scene.

Randy was directly behind her, walking in her

footsteps as they neared the box.

It was a rather large box, about the size of a large packing box from UPS. Brown with some letters on the side facing up, they were smudged with watermarks. The box was tipped over, lying on one side. A few contents from the box looked like they had spilled out and as she moved closer, her stomach started to turn.

She noticed a purple ribbon and the blue jeans near the open face of the box. The jeans appeared to have bloodstains on it. Hopefully, those are just dirty water stains. She hoped. Edging closer, she pulled out her latex gloves and made her way to the opposite side of the box. She was careful not to touch anything more than she needed to and careful not to step on anything in the grass. "Something - EX Industries; Meacon Bend, New York," Terri read the business name on the box.

The paper was torn, and a portion of the name was missing. *He had on blue jeans, sweatshirt, and a purple ribbon, a rag of some sort.* She mentally inventoried the items leading up to the box.

Walking her way around the box to the blind side, *Oh, my God,* Terri's mind raced. *Is that a real hand? A human hand?* For a moment she thought she might get sick from the empty pit in her stomach. *This better be a sick-fucking joke.*

She recalled how she and David put fake blood in Mike's shampoo bottle as a Halloween joke last year. Mike screamed like a little girl on a Ferris wheel as he jetted down the hall at the precinct wearing nothing but a towel over his head! *Damn, that was funny.* Terri let out a nervous sigh thinking about it.

She delicately pulled at the box to see if it would open for further inspection, her hopes of an injured raccoon now gone. *Oh God, it is a hand and a man.*

The odor of decaying flesh made her nostrils flare. Her face was white as paper as she saw the head and arm of a dark-haired man jammed into the box. The body was twisted and folded with no signs of life.

"Jesus Terri," Randy muttered out loud. He

hadn't seen human remains since he returned from Iraq and he was suddenly feeling the zing of distant memories. They backed away from the stench and toward the road.

"Mike, would you get started on the photographs, please? Black and white and also color film?" Terri instructed, out of habit. "Mike. Mike! Stop staring and start taking pictures. We are going to need a few before we try to find identification," Terri's voice was calm and confident.

"What the fuck?" Terri said as she wondered how a body could fit into a box this size.

She stood there, prioritizing her thoughts. The body of a dead person is like an encyclopedia of information, and she had to obtain as much of it as possible. She was a little overwhelmed.

Terri left Mike to take his pictures and walked back toward the truck for a larger notebook so she could begin jotting down a few of her own notes. Once the pictures were taken, they could move the body and try to find identification.

"Randy, while Mike is finishing up, could you see if there are any other witnesses and conduct the interviews? I am going call the Captain and the Medical Examiner to get them started our way."

"Terri, I know, but there are no witnesses, just the Johnson boy on the bike and he only said he found the box and some clothing. He didn't say if he saw anything else, but he is just a kid," Randy was hoping he would have had a more significant assignment.

"Randy, go talk to the kid and his parents. We will need all the information he has. I want to know if he walked up to the box or touched anything. When did he first noticed the box? Was it there yesterday? You know, as much as he can give us," she was interrupted by the sight of the Channel 44 News truck barreling down toward them, the dust from the road was flying.

"Who the hell let these guys in?" Terri demanded of Randy, pointing to the news crew, "See if we can get

51

the road blocked off at Highway 612 until we are done out here."

"They must have heard it on the scanner Terri. I'm sorry, I forgot about roping off the road after we talked and then you showed up," Randy tried to explain as he looked down at his feet, the embarrassment glowing in his cheeks.

The reporter stopped short of Terri's Tahoe, startled by Duke as he let out a deep penetrating bark. "Melissa, you are going to have to move the news truck back, please. Move it to the end of the road, if you don't mind. And take your news friends with you. This is not the time," Terri instructed. She wished David were home from vacation; he had a way with the media. David could put a spin on any story to make it sound like this was not a big deal.

She threw a hard look at Jones, "Randy, at least get some crime scene tape up. Wrap it from your car to my truck until we get these guys back, please," Terri ordered.

Again, she wished David Cooper were there. She had been assigned to work with David nearly a year ago after his wife and daughter were killed in a horrific crash. He had retreated since then, absorbed with his new 'gaming' hobby. He sure did know how to do an investigation though, rarely missed a thing. His OCD seemed worse than Mike's. Although his personality sucked. He was difficult to read, and most of the time he was a self-centered jerk. As she looked around, she recalled that the crash was not too far from where they were now.

"Who is this guy? I need to look at his clothing and body for stains, laundry marks, monograms, tattoos," her voice trailed as she mumbled to herself.

She pulled out her phone to make some calls. 3 missed calls. There were two from Ryann and one from David. *I'll call her when I get time; she is going to love this.* Terri dialed the Medical Examiner.

"Mike, take shots of the road and photograph

everything, all the way to the body," Terri instructed. She pointed and signaled while she was on hold waiting for the Medical Examiner.

"Yep. I'll start back at the bend in the road and walk all the way. I'll get 360 photos for the file. And of course, I will get some close-ups," Pierce said, excited about using his new toy.

"Okay, Captain Williams is on her way. The medical examiner is on the other side of the county; he will be here in about 45 minutes. That gives us time to do our part."

"Terri, I didn't see a wallet on this guy. No identification," Pierce informed her, "at least not until we turn the body."

"Okay, we'll just have to order fingerprinting, DNA tests, and dental X-rays to see if we can't get this guy identified," Terri reviewed her notes, ensuring everything had been adequately documented. "If we have to, we'll get a forensic artist to do a composite; maybe the public will know who he is," she voiced the option. "If you are done with photos, let me run Duke around a bit and see if we can find anything else," she told Pierce.

She took Duke from his back seat cage and let him pee. When he finished, she gave him swift commands and watched him turn circles then sit at her feet. She attached the 25-foot lead to his collar and led him to the first boot on the shoulder, "Here, boy. Here," she pointed to the shoe.

Duke put his nose to the ground and sniffed around. Soon enough he had a scent and followed it all the way to the box. He stopped and sat down. Terri pulled him and pointed to the ground again as she walked him around the box. Once more, Duke circled the box then sat, just as he was trained to do when the trail went cold.

"This is where the trail ends. I'm betting whoever dropped the box out here walked straight from the area where we are parked, dumped it, and then walked directly back."

Duke gave no other indications. She called Cooper back while they waited for the Captain and Medical Examiner. He didn't answer so she left a message, still wishing he were there to deal with the media. He had a media kind of face; at least he believed he did.

It wasn't long before the Captain arrived and Terri was filling her in. The M.E. arrived and completed necessary verifications, but could not determine a cause of death at the scene.

When the M.E. assistants removed the body for transport to the morgue, they located his wallet and a set of car keys. A small black bi-fold wallet contained $159.00 in cash, a Meijer receipt, and a business card.

Chapter 5

Ryann's car was parked in the driveway close to the garage door. Pulling in she noticed the bathroom light was on,

"Ryann must still be up," Terri thought out loud, "she never leaves the bathroom light on." Terri looked down at her watch, after midnight already. *What a day.*

"Come on, Duke," she beckoned for her canine as she opened the door and he gave a much-needed squat at the edge of the drive.

"Let's go!" She called after him as he took off in a dead sprint towards the shadows at the perimeter of her property, barking.

"Duke! Here!" She reluctantly gave him the work command that snapped him from the playful pet that he was into the fiercely trained tracking partner. He stopped obediently in his tracks and did an abrupt about-face, racing towards her. Such a harsh voice command from his handler meant to leave the situation alone.

Terri opened the door and let him in. He ran by her and into the kitchen for a drink.

"Ryann?" She called shutting the door behind her. Remembering the bathroom light, Terri called for Duke once again.

"Duke," he sensed her mild insecurity and glued himself to the side of her leg as she turned on the hall light that led down to the bathroom. The bathroom door was shut, and the bath radio was playing softly. It was something from a retro- station and it sounded like Barry Manilow.

"And you came, and you gave without taking...Oh Mandy," the words softly trailed. She stood at the door listening beyond the music, and after several moments she heard the soft sound of moving water.

She looked at Duke, who had his ears tilted at the door, bent with an alertness Terri recognized as one of familiarity. Reading her dog as only she could, the person in the bath obviously did not make him feel threatened.

He continued to sniff the lower edge of the door as a murmuring hum drowned out the silky lull of Barry's voice, "You kissed me and stopped me from shaking, and I need you today, Oh Mandy."

The voice blended into a duet singing along with Barry. Terri paused, and then quietly began untying her boots. Leaving her jacket, keys, and wallet in a pile on the floor, she inaudibly ordered Duke to sit and stay pointing to the floor. He took his position upon her clothes in his usual protective manner but snuggled in for a probable extended stay near the door.

Terri hesitated and took a long slow drawn breath before opening the door. As she did, the steam from the bath enveloped her body and invited her in.

Ryann was submerged in the bath; hair soaked and streaked back, bubbles encapsulating her shoulders as she lay in the oversized Jacuzzi tub soaking up the warmth of the water.

"It's about time you arrived home... I have been waiting for you," Ryann spoke softly.

Terri didn't notice the candles lit, filling the room with the humid rainforest odor. She was fixated on her bareness. "You are so beautiful," she breathed.

"Come, sit with me, please. Tell me about your day. You haven't texted or called me all day," Ryann's voice was soft and wispy, as she swirled the water near her thigh.

Terri sat next to the tub and grabbed a loofa sponge, dipping it into the water. The heat in the bathroom kept her from getting cold, but the anticipation of possibly getting into the bathtub warmed her to the bottoms of her feet.

"No, silly, please... in here" Ryann wanted her. She had been waiting for Terri all night; she tenderly waved the bubbles, coaxing her into the water. There was plenty of room for two, as if by design, the tub extra long and was a perfect fit.

"No, you look like you've been in here too long already," she was oblivious to the intent of the invite, her mind spinning.

She began unconsciously soaping up the sponge and knelt next to the tub. Terri started on the right foot. She scrubbed the loofa across the top of her foot then under her toes. Her left hand slid up and down along her calf as she gripped the sponge and spun it around to her ankle. The smoothness of Ryann's freshly shaven leg made the sponge glide effortlessly.

Ryann grabbed her by the shoulders and pulled her closer. Her arm plunged into the water, keeping her from falling in; it splashed up over the sidewalls.

Ryann was playful and pushed her back from the water. Just as quickly as she had pushed her, Ryann grasped onto her shoulders and pulled them toward her face; Terri's lips met hers, and they kissed.

The kiss was firm, and Terri felt herself grow heated, but hesitant- her mind shifted back to work scenarios, and she tensed.

Sensing her reservation and distraction, Ryann stopped short of pulling her into the tub, hoping it was work, she thought she was finally breaking Terri's protective layer.

"Honey, why don't you just talk to me about your evening? It is late, and I've been in the bath so long I'm crinkling up," she giggled.

She climbed out while Terri dutifully cloaked her with a towel, "Did you see the news today?"

"I got a couple of missed calls from you, and I thought you had already heard about what happened today," Terri dried her back and handed her the folded pajama pants and t-shirt left on the sink.

"I really haven't had much time, I did see a flash on my laptop that there was breaking news in the area, but I really didn't see the piece. I was on a conference call, and then I forgot about it. What was it? Are you ok?" Ryann asked.

"Yeah, that news flash was probably about Waterford. We found a man in a box out on Stern Creek Road."

"What?" Ryann asked, "A man in a box?"

Terri felt she failed to recognize the seriousness of the statement, "Yes, a man. I mean, well. He was dead. Obviously." Terri appeared anxious and began rambling as they exited the bathroom back toward the kitchen.

"Like what kind of box? Was the man chopped in pieces? Who was it? Who, who found him? How old was he?" Ryann sat at the kitchen table brushing her hair.

Terri was rummaging through the refrigerator and grabbed a beer. She sat next to her, but only for a moment. She was back up and pacing, getting a glass, pouring the beer, back to the refrigerator.

"Sit, sit for a second," Ryann stood up and pulled the chair out. "Or would you rather talk in bed? Never mind, come on, let's get you changed and settled down."

Ryann picked up the beverage and grabbed Terri by the arm, "Come on honey. Was Randy there? And Mike? Was David back today? Where did you say you found him?" She was asking so many questions.

"So far a mystery Ryann. He's like 35, and he isn't from here, at least I didn't recognize him. He had a wallet, but no identification. It might be a lover's quarrel, an ex-husband. He might be on Randy's hunt list, or a reported missing person, or a gang member from out of town," Terri thinking out loud about whom this guy might be.

"Lover's quarrel? The hunt list?" Ryann asked.

"Yeah, you know a jealous husband. Hunt list. That's the list of sex offenders Randy and Mike were tracking down because they didn't verify their addresses. So he could be one of the guys on the list."

"Guess you wouldn't have to find him then…. Sorry, not funny," Ryann was trying to ease some of her tension.

Terri cracked a smile, "Yeah, I guess you are right. But we really don't know who he is or how he was killed. So we don't have any suspects either. We don't know if he was married or if he had kids. We couldn't do the next of kin notification so all that will have to wait too. That also means we can't let the news know anything happened because we don't have a name. Mike took a shit ton of pictures and Randy will roll his fingerprints at the morgue tomorrow. We can send the prints in, hopefully, he is in the system," Terri explained, and then took a big gulp of her beer.

"System?" Ryann asked. She tended to key in on certain words.

"Yes, for any criminal offenses. That might be the only way we will know who he is, through his criminal history. Honestly, I hope it does come up with something, so we don't have to reconstruct his face."

"How do you think this guy died? Could you tell? Was he shot?" Ryann was asking more about the dead man.

"He still had his wallet and cash on him. I don't think it was a robbery. I don't know exactly what he did, but I don't know why that would matter. I'm not sure he deserved what happened to him. He is dead now, and we don't have much to go on. There are no houses near that curve on Stern Creek, but tomorrow we will know from the crime lab who the dead man is, and we can go from there. Maybe they will be able to find some trace evidence from his clothing. And there was one receipt. From the Meijer here in town, like from two nights ago," Terri talked about their only evidence thus far.

"Does that mean anything? What did the receipt say? What did he buy?" Ryann prodded.

"I'm not sure yet. Maybe we can check some video surveillance and see if he was there with anyone or if he has a car still in the parking lot. Or maybe someone dropped him off. Something. I'm tired hon. I have so many things on my mind right now," Terri leaned back in the bed, but Ryann continued.

"What did Randy say about it? And Mike? Did you guys have your meeting this morning? How did that go?"

Terri finished the last sip and lay down. Her thoughts swirled around the dead man.

"It looked like he was strangled or something. There was a huge black and blue mark on his neck, and it looked puffed up, but maybe the guy just had a fat neck. Maybe strangulation. That would take a pretty big suspect, one that was pretty damn strong too," she was developing the profile of the killer.

"He wasn't wearing his shoes, but whoever dumped him, also dumped one of his shoes, so we can assume he had taken them off. Maybe there is trace evidence on the bottoms of his socks."

"Shoe? As opposed to shoes?" Ryann asked about the second shoe.

"Yes, 'shoe.' There was only one. We didn't find the other one."

"There were a couple of ribbons; purple, silver, and gold ones. Like the kind you might use to wrap a wedding gift. Weird. It's a puzzle so far. And then there was the box. The name was smudged off, but the box could have been randomly used. Or maybe it was a statement," Terri stared at the ceiling while she spoke.

"I think we are going to have an early start tomorrow. We have to find out where that box came from. There must be some type of postmark on it somewhere. David will be there tomorrow, too, and we can fill him in with what we know. Maybe he can offer a fresh set of eyes and some new insight," Terri's eyes grew heavier with stress.

"David never showed up? Wasn't he supposed to be at your meeting this morning? Why wouldn't he be there? Weak stomach?" She was trying to make Terri think about it, but she was already lost in thought.

Sensing she might be drifting too far away from the conversation, she asked another crime scene question, "A real mystery, huh? What about tire tracks, or trash, or..."

Terri cut her off again, "This isn't CSI; we can't just run a tire track and say it came from a Ford or a Dodge. We don't just run driver's licenses, and some special computer brings up a map of every location where they had ever lived, or their neighborhoods, or their friends. In fact, we have nothing like that at all. That is all cinematic bullshit."

"Okay, okay. It's okay. You guys are good detectives, and you will figure it out. Try to get some rest so you can function tomorrow," Ryann saw that it apparently had Terri worn, both mentally and physically.

"Seriously, it isn't like we can take a piece of chewed up gum and come up with DNA that will tell us who the killer was. Especially with nothing – I mean, we don't even have a piece of chewed up gum!"

Ryann lowered her voice, "Alright, I've got it. Relax. Get some sleep. I will wake you when I get up before I leave," and set the alarm for 5 am.

Chapter 6

The day was longer than she anticipated and Terri did not make time for anything other than work. She had been in meetings all day with Jones, Pierce, and Cooper. They were busy working on theories about the homicide, but that was all they had. They were in the waiting stages. Waiting for the laboratory results, they were waiting for the public to say something, waiting for someone to be reported missing.

Jones had left Jess a message, and she had not gotten back to him. In the meantime, they were sorting out the daily tasks and developing the residential verifications for the sex offender list.

They planned on making the Monica Street address a priority, just to scratch it from their list of things to do, but somehow the day had gotten away from them, and it was already getting dark.

Terri finally realized the time, and it occurred to her she hadn't even spoken with Ryann. She called her and left a message on her cell phone. *She'll be pissed; it's already after 10.*

She needed some fresh air and decided to take a drive out to Stern Creek Road to imagine what she may be missing. *The answer would be in the details*, Terri thought. Perhaps she could see something she had not noticed before; maybe there was some clue they had forgotten to pick up.

The boys had parted ways, and while Jones and Pierce headed to Bob's, Cooper went home to meet his 'gamer' buds.

She had been driving the area for a bit, gotten out and checked the area where the box was found but didn't notice anything unusual, so she decided to head home.

There was a 'one-eye' headed toward her on the

normally desolate road of Highway 612. Terri slowed and pulled to the side of the road and waited to make a U-turn on the vehicle.

Initiating the traffic stop for the violation, she approached guarded and deliberately slow. She had her patrol vehicle spotlight posted on the center inside rearview mirror, illuminating most of the interior of the vehicle. The vehicle was a rental vehicle registered out of Ludington, New York.

"License, registration, and your proof of insurance, please," Terri asked as she cautiously scanned the interior of the vehicle with one eye and kept the other on the driver. She took unconscious mental inventory of the contents; she noted small cardboard boxes; taped-up, labeled 'Ross, Inc.', a suitcase, and a briefcase.

She also noted a Crash Reconstructionist magazine flipped onto the back seat, camera equipment, laser sights, and distance measuring tools.

The front seat had strands of gift-wrap and bows, a card of some type, a pair of leather gloves, and a map of the area.

"I'm sorry, I didn't realize I was speeding. It is just that I am on my way through and I," the woman started. Terri watched her as she leaned over toward the glove box to look for her paperwork.

Conducting another, more personal type of inventory scan, she started at the driver's feet; she couldn't help but think 'nice legs'.

She must have been about 35 years old, 5'8", 135, and her bra fit perfectly causing her breasts to round out like two soft oranges stuffed into the skintight white cashmere. She could see the lacing in paisley print pressed into the sweater. *Left hand, no ring.*

"Here you go, I am so sorry, I am just on my way through, I, uh, was following this map, and I guess I wasn't paying attention," her words melted into the air as Terri caught herself staring into her ocean blue eyes. Her shoulder length sandy brown hair swept alongside her shoulder seemed like silk. Her clear skin appeared as though she had just peeled herself out of a magazine.

"Not your speed, you have a head light out, Miss Ross. What brings you out this way?" Terri was reading from her New York driver's license, noticing the picture did not do her justice. She barely noticed the insurance was for a personal vehicle, Christine Kisne and it had recently expired.

Terri looked over the license and saw those ocean blues again. She glanced down and watched as Allison Ross nervously rubbed the top of her knee. Terri noticed the skirt was barely long enough to cover her underwear as she sat in the vehicle and speculated they might be black and lace.

About 3 inches from her hip she assumed. It was only long enough to make the skirt look like it was 100% cotton and dried a few times too many. She wondered how firm her legs were after wearing those heels all day.

"Allison Ross," the woman introduced herself and grabbed a business card that was handily available in a cubby to the left of the steering wheel.

"Patterson and Ross. We represent the critically injured and their family representatives in car crashes," she explained.

The words flowed as if she was reading from cue cards for a commercial, "I'm on the investigative end of the business. I find myself traveling to various locations as part of my employment. It seems I'm never in one place long enough to remember the roads."

Terri looked down at it, for a moment forgetting that she was a police officer and had initiated a traffic stop on a desolate stretch of road for an equipment violation.

"So you're a lawyer? It is an odd time of the night for you to be out by Stern Creek Road. Almost no one travels this way, and certainly not this late. It's nearly 11:30 pm," Terri was flirting with her as she looked down at her watch.

She had been looking forward to a cold beer.

However, the desire wasn't as strong as it was to stand in the night wind getting more personal information from Miss Ross. But she had promised Trisha she would meet her at work.

Allison stammered, reading from Terri's nametag, "Uhh, actually, Officer Bradford, I am a little lost."

"Where exactly are you looking to go?" Terri sensed her embarrassment and wondered if she was checking her out as she had just done. She wondered if her uniform made her look fat and if her hair looked all right.

Terri handed the license and information back without noting it on her daily activity sheet.

"I was trying to get to the Hampton Inn. I was following this damn GPS, but somehow it led me here, and I don't see anything that looks like a hotel. Perhaps you could give me directions?" She asked and looked down the road and then back.

She smiled and gathered herself, "The only Hampton Inn is about 30 miles from here near the freeway, but I can point you in the right direction."

Terri started with directions that would take her back toward the main road, "Have a good night ma'am, and you can pick up a bulb if you stop at the hardware store tomorrow." Terri turned to walk back to her patrol vehicle in the usual fashion, side-stepping while keeping an eye on the driver.

"Officer?" Allison leaned her head out the window and yelled back toward Terri.

Startled, Terri re-approached the vehicle, "Yes, ma'am?"

"Do you have a business card? A number where I can reach you? I... I may be by this way again sometime soon, and perhaps I could call you for some directional assistance?" Allison said nervously, her cheeks rosy and eyes looking everywhere but up.

Without thinking, Terri unbuttoned her shirt pocket and pulled out a business card. Her name was written in bold letters across the middle, and Waterford

Police Department printed in the lower right corner with a contact number.

"I can always be reached at this number, but if you need to get a hold of me, here is my cell phone," Terri flipped the card over and wrote her personal number on the back.

She thought about calling Ryann on her way back to the patrol vehicle, but when she opened the door, the radio was already chirping.

"3742- status check," the dispatcher bellowed.

"I'm clear and still headed for out of service," Terri spoke into the hand mic. She was already halfway home.

She caged Duke and changed before heading out to meet Trish. She was already pulling into Bob's bar when she remembered to call Ryann. She decided to hurry and call before she went in. Trisha would be waiting for her with the usual tall draft, extra cold, just the way she liked it.

"Hello?" Ryann answered, she sounded half asleep.

"Hi, babe. Did I wake you?" Terri asked, half out of concern and somewhat hoping she had not. "Are you at your apartment?" Terri didn't know if she wanted her to be at her house or not, but either way, she was going to stay out and have a beer.

"No, well, I laid down about an hour ago," she sounded interrupted and slightly irritated.

"Oh, I just wanted to call and let you know I was stopping at the bar to meet up with Trish. She is closing tonight, and I seem to be wide awake," Terri informed her.

"Okay, how did the meeting go? Do you have any ideas about the murder? Did you get the lab reports yet?" Ryann seemed to be waking up.

Terri didn't answer any of the questions instead Ryann waited another moment before stating, "Alright then, call me tomorrow when you are free?" Ryann sounded more hopeful than polite.

"Ok. Goodnight," Terri shut the engine to the car

off and walked into the bar.

"Good evening, my friend!" Trisha already had the draft mug, frozen and topped.

"This is exactly what I needed," she pulled out the bar stool and grabbed the drink as she sat. "Thank you," half the mug was emptied on the first swallow.

"Wow, tough day Terri?" Trisha asked.

"Not so bad, today. In fact, the day ended rather nicely," Terri referenced the last traffic stop of the evening. Trisha was washing down the back counters and drying the last of the glasses.

"What was so nice about it?" She did not turn to look. Instead, she grabbed the Windex and began wiping the bar mirror near the splash sink. "It's been slow in here tonight, and I am so ready to get out of here," she continued working.

"We have been really busy trying to develop some clues on that homicide. I mean, I even asked Randy to ask his friend to help us on this one. We might have to ask the state crime lab to re-evaluate our stuff just in case Mike, and I missed something at the crime scene. I hope we didn't, well at least I didn't. Right now, we have nothing. But today things were getting back to normal. It was life as usual throughout the day, you know, speeding teenagers, a couple of older couples passing through, and lastly, a beauty driving a BMW," Terri set the mug down and slid it over toward Trisha for a refill.

"A what? Did you just say 'beauty in a BMW'?" They both laughed. She placed the refilled mug on the counter and pushed it back toward Terri, "You want some popcorn?" Trisha was emptying the kernels from the last batch.

"Yeah, but only if you are making some," Terri never turned down fresh popcorn.

"I have to; we're still open another three hours. Everyone that walks in here likes hot popcorn. For that matter, it doesn't matter if it's hot, as long as they have popcorn. Sometimes I think this machine gets more use than the tap," Trisha smiled and readied the oil and butter flavoring, she wanted to know more about the murder, but Terri would talk to her about it when she was ready.

"Now, about this 'beauty'?" Terri couldn't hide her smile as she began, "Well..."

"Uh oh...I take it we aren't talking about Ryann?" Trisha recalled how Terri spoke of her a few months back when Terri happened to meet a 'beauty' named Ryann.

"It's nothing really," Terri said as she started on her second glass.

"You know, I don't think Ryann is your type anyway. She is kind of different. I mean, I have only met her a couple of times, and she seemed so possessive. She's never been to the bar with you. Does she even drink?" Trisha was in a mood, but Ryann had taken her best bud away, and Terri had just recently been coming back around again.

"Trish, she isn't 'different.' She just doesn't party, and she has her own business that keeps her occupied," Terri defended her.

"Well, you don't talk about her much, and I don't know anything about her. I thought you were getting serious about this one?" The last patron left the bar, and Trisha poured herself a short glass of brew.

"She has had a rough life. I'm proud of her, actually. Her parents are dead; her brother is in the military, somewhere overseas. She said her sister was killed in a motor vehicle crash and she has had a hard time processing. I guess they were very close. She stays a little detached, but I don't blame her, I might too if I lost everyone that was important to me," Terri told her.

"Wow. Where is Ryann from?" Trisha asked. "Is she planning on staying, like how is the dating going?"

Terri finished her drink, "I don't know. I'm still learning about her and her business. Some consulting business but she said it is a private firm. I think she said it was based in New York, or New Jersey, New something. C-MET or something like that."

"Sea Met? What is that?" Trish asked.

"I don't know, I thought something to do with counseling management something-something," Terri was guessing, she had never really asked her.

They both laughed again. Trish finished her short and poured another, offering Terri a third, "No, I have to drive. I'll have a diet coke. Thanks."

The automated jukebox lulled in the background as Trish sat back down, "What's the word on the street?" Terri asked about the town gossip.

"Ha, ha! Word on the street is no one knows where that dead guy came from. Word is he was a child molester and got what he deserved. Someone mentioned some muddy hunting boots that were used to drag the body through the marsh before dumping him in the trees," Trisha repeated barroom chatter.

"They said he did time for molesting a cops daughter and the cop never got over it. Probably got his revenge stabbing the asshole in the chest 25 times."

"Oh, Jesus! Trish, the guy wasn't stabbed! For God's sake, and he wasn't dragged anywhere or wearing hunting boots! Who comes up with this shit?" Terri shook her head. The rumors around town would have this guy a martyr before too long. But she realized they would have to find a way to get this murder solved, and they would have to do it before the whole town became unsettled.

Chapter 7

The offices were unusually quiet when Jones walked into the detective cubicles. It was Saturday, and Jack had weekends off. He made a fresh pot of coffee and helped himself to the first 8 ounces out of the pot and a day-old bagel for the microwave.

Nice and quiet in here, he thought. *Finally, I can sort through some of this mounting paperwork and get a head start for Monday.* It had been a few days since the murder, and so many items had been pushed to the bottom of his list, he decided it was best to come in on his own time to get things done. He was hoping Jessica had not only sent him an email with a workup on his two offenders. Kevin Kramer and George Moore. He had given her another name, Jeremy Hines, but only because his mother was looking for him.

He was also waiting for the laboratory reports on the dead guy in the box, but Jones knew those results would go directly to Terri when they came in.

He poked his head around his cube and eyed her desk. *She's not here yet. Maybe later. Maybe later today.* He really wanted to discuss the cases with her and see what she thought they might do next. He was sure she would come in today, she nearly always came in on Saturday when they had important things to do.

Jones decided he would start with his email. He searched for anything from her, anxious to start reading what she had come up with on the Monica Street address for Moore.

He sorted through a variety of police notices, amber alert information, and legal updates. *Damn, nothing from Jess.* He found himself reading an article from an Accident Reconstruction magazine about staged crashes he found interesting. By the time he finished reading it, he was ready for another cup of coffee.

Jones hadn't realized he didn't put enough water

in the pot, but he didn't mind the sludge. *Whoa, good thing you aren't here today Jack, this is thick stuff,* he chuckled.

He returned to his desk and began shuffling the paperwork when he clicked the voicemail to speakerphone.

"Randy, it's Jessica. I started a work-up on your guys and found something you may think is very interesting. It looks like both offenders, Hines and Moore, used the same address. That one you gave me on Monica Street- 51172. Moore had a previous address on Oak Street, but that was three months ago. He recently verified from your office."

She continued, "I drove by there, and a vehicle registered to him was parked on the road near the driveway, so most likely he is there. Hines has not verified or changed his address since last year. Maybe he is there, too, but he doesn't have any vehicles on record so I couldn't look for it when I did the drive-by. Anyway, I'm still working on the other one, Kramer. He is a little harder to find. Call me, and we can set up a time to go over it. Talk soon, Jess," Jessica's voicemail was clear and confident.

Damn, you are a good woman, he found himself smiling at the thought of her.

Still, at his desk, he changed lines on the phone and called Terri. "Hey Terri, it is Randy. Call me. I think we may want to visit that house Monica Street today, if you are coming in. I mean the guy who said he lived on Monica? Jess said he was there. Interestingly, she also said our other offender Hines, had also used that address. Call me back."

He kept the secret of doing some private research on Kramer. He had a habit of cluttering things up by trying to answer too many questions at once without waiting for answers from the last question. He also didn't like to share any of his information.

He wanted to be the one to find him so he could tell his mother she overreacted and there had been nothing to worry about. That way she would quit calling every registration period wondering if he had come in.

Jones was anxious to start moving in the murder investigation, and his next call was back to Jess. There was no answer, so he left a message.

"What are you guys working on today?" David Cooper walked back to the cubes.

"I'm not sure yet Coop, didn't know you were coming in today," Jones was a little startled. He thought Cooper was a bit odd and when they tried to discuss any of the sex offender investigations, he would get up and walk away. Jones chalked it up to his style, some cops like investigating check fraud and writing traffic tickets, some cops like solving a real crime – like homicide and rape.

"I need to get my patrol car out of the garage and head over to an address on Monica Street to check out a sex offender," Jones gave Cooper minimal information about his pending investigations.

"Pierce and I made it as far as the street sign before being re-routed to another call," he tried to tell him.

Cooper was already busy logging into his personal laptop, "Hmm," he managed to respond. He was strategically placing a small ceramic trinket on his desk near an old photo of his daughter. Looked like a dancing bear, Jones instantly thought of Cooper's deceased daughter and looked away.

Saved by the phone, Jones picked up the ringing line, "Hi Terri. Thanks for calling me back. I was hoping you were coming in today and we could go check an address on Monica Street," he read the caller identification. Jones was telling more than asking, but Terri wasn't biting.

"I have to get my grass cut and do some grocery shopping. My friend and I have some plans tomorrow; maybe we can get started first thing Monday morning?"

Terri didn't talk about Ryann much, at Ryann's request. She rarely spoke about her 'dates' with her co-workers. Instead, they only understood she wasn't settled down, nor would she be.

"I guess I can wait until Monday; I have to cut my grass too. But I think I will do a drive-by anyway if that's okay?" Jones was going to do it anyway. He also planned on calling Jess to see if she would be willing to meet up tonight or tomorrow.

"Okay, you are right. We need a break anyway while we wait for the lab results," Jones was disappointed but already devising his plan for Monday.

Monday came quickly, and Jones was already preparing to leave the office, "Guess that means you are bringing me lunch today instead of a break?" Jack asked as he watched him load his patrol vehicle.

"Honestly, I hope I am back in time for the mail, or at least the UPS delivery. I'm taking Pierce, too. What do you want for lunch? You know Pierce, he will want to stop on the way there and back," he picked up the phone and dialed Pierce.

"Pierce, are you almost here?" He asked into the mouthpiece. "I've got an address we need to check and Jack wants us to grab him some lunch. Ok, see you in a few, I'll walk out when you pull up. Thanks," he readied for the ride to Monica Street.

Jack knew he would be stuck all day at the office, and decided to place his lunch order, "I'll phone you if anything shows up before you get back. You guys stopping by Amanda's? I could use a couple of chicken tacos."

"3742, can you take a call?" Dispatch inquired.

"Stand by one," Terri answered the radio while completing her search for a place to set her coffee, "go ahead."

"Can you make 51172 Monica Street? Officers are at that residence verifying an address and aren't getting an answer. The neighbors said they found the side garage door open, but the owners are supposed to be out of town. Wondering if you could bring your dog by?"

"Sure, you can show me in route," Terri found picked her coffee up and sipped. *Assholes couldn't wait 30 minutes for me to get to work and go with them.* She knew Jones was not the kind of guy to sit still.

Terri had stopped near an abandoned farm property at the edge of town to let Duke out to run before heading in. Before summoning him back to the vehicle, she called Ryann. There was no answer, so she left a message. *She is busier than I am,* Terri thought.

"Sorry, Duke, we can't stay. I wish we could; we have another call buddy," Terri apologetically explained.

Her phone rang, "Terri," she answered.

"Officer Bradford? This is Allison Ross. Are you busy?"

Terri held her breath, "Um, no. I mean, yes. Is everything okay? Would it be possible to call you back?" She had mixed feelings; *should I hang up and talk later, or talk know and let the call wait?* Allison was making her a bit nervous.

"Oh yes. Everything is fine. Call me when you get some time, maybe later this evening? I have a couple of questions about a crash I am investigating," Terri imagined Allison slanting her head, pulling her hair back with slow blinking mannerisms. She was difficult to deny, with that soft voice. She envisioned her deep inviting eyes.

"I'm on my way to a possible track. I shouldn't be too long, but either way, I will call you back," Terri was wondering how it might be possible for them to meet up.

A warm sensation flooded her body, like a long shot of hot damn, making its way to her stomach; the warmth filled her fingertips and toes.

Allison responded, "I have some research to do and phone calls to make. I will be at the local library. I'll have my phone on vibrate so you can call me. I am looking forward to it."

Terri took that as an invite, and she hung up. Of course, she wants to meet with me, she reflected for a mere moment before pushing the thought out of her mind and continuing to 51172 Monica Street.

Arriving at the address, she saw Jones and Pierce. Terri stopped short of their patrol unit and exited. She paused long enough to adjust her gun belt.

"We knocked on the door, but no answer," Jones informed her. "The neighbor came out and told us they hadn't been home in about a month. They live here for the summer and visit their children for months on end. The neighbor to the north said he noticed the side garage door open the other day. A little while later, the door was closed again."

"Other than that, he said he hadn't seen anything or anyone unusual around," Pierce added his two cents.

"We asked if he knew the man that lives here, but he said the man is older and married. They don't have young kids that stay at home, at least he hadn't seen any."

"So what brought you guys out here this morning?" Terri asked, "And why do you need Duke?" Her questions were fair, if only because it seemed to be a simple address check.

"Well, this guy came in to register as a sex offender at this address. Pierce and I were here a few weeks ago on a breaking and entering alarm, but there was no sign of a breaking and entering, and no one answered the door. I thought the house was for sale, but it isn't. The neighbor just told us that the owners had been out of town then, too," Jones said.

"You mean, that neighbor?" Terri asked pointing at the man on the sidewalk.

"Yeah, his name is John something, John Glover I think. I'll get his information again in a minute."

Jones continued despite the interruption, "The weird thing is a man came in last week trying to register at this address, but I told him he had the wrong address because Pierce and I had just been there."

"He insisted that he lived here, and then I gave the information to Jess and she was able to verify that he was supposed to be here. Anyway, it is only address verification at this point, but he is on my list. I think the dude was shady and full of shit."

"I'm not sure why you think he wouldn't be here, Randy? Maybe he is at work?" Terri suggested.

"His address checks out here, and his car is parked on the road, but it is down the street, not even close to the driveway," Jones started to explain why he needed to verify Moore today, and not come back tomorrow.

"This guy gave me the creeps when he came in, something isn't right. I think the guy was up to something, Terri. I mean, we've been out here and now he is supposed to be here and no one is answering. I think he has something to hide."

Pierce pointed out the contradiction between the information gleaned from the neighbor and the address verification, "Glover says no one lives here but an older couple. I doubt they would leave their house open for squatters."

Terri turned her attention to Pierce as he took over the conversation and continued, "Jarhead gave me the file last week. I ran a law enforcement check on the name and address of the Moore guy. He has been using this address to verify for about three months."

Jones interrupted, "The other people associated with the address are the homeowners, Mr. and Mrs. Donnelly. According to the neighbors, they are the only ones they ever see here, and that gives me enough probable cause to get in there and look around."

"Jarhead, patience, have some patience," Pierce remarked.

Pierce explained to Terri how and why he checked the occupants of the address, "According to the Secretary of State Bureau of Driver's License, someone by the name of Hines lived here at one point, but his driver's license had not been renewed. It expired last year."

Terri was intrigued by the information.

"Anyway, Jarhead called me, and we came out here. There was no answer at the door. We went around back, and all of the doors are locked, and the windows are secure."

Pierce continued, "The side garage door is unlocked, but the inside door is locked. It looks like everything is here. I mean, it doesn't appear that anyone made entry and all of the tools are still hung neatly on the pegboard." The outlines of the tools were made in thick black marker in the event someone forgot where they went.

Looking around, Terri noticed the same things. The tools were placed perfectly, and nothing appeared to be missing. The push mower and edger were in place. An expensive generator was tucked into the corner. It didn't look like anything was disturbed in here anyway.

Nodding, Terri agreed with Jones and Pierce. "Did you try knocking?" Terri asked half joking and forgetting if they told her.

"We knocked with no answer. We tried to look into the windows, but the curtains are drawn. We did a basic look of the periphery and didn't notice any footprints, hand smudges, or pry marks on any of the windows or doors," Jones had looked for food bowls and outdoor kennels as part of his preliminary investigation.

"There doesn't appear to be any animals inside or even kept outside, and the neighbors confirm that," Jones tried to impress Terri with his investigative skills.

"What did the neighbor say about there being any vehicles in the driveway?" Terri questioned.

"He hasn't seen any, and he watches diligently," Jones told her.

Terri glanced Glover's way and decided he probably had nothing better to do. He was a short squinty guy with horned rim glasses.

"Mr. Glover, have you seen anyone strange in the neighborhood?" Jones asked again, just to see if he had changed his story. Jones can be abrasive at times and didn't exactly encourage others to share information with him.

Scratching his head, he responded, "No. Not really, nothing out of the ordinary. Just you cops drivin' around checkin' us out. I thought one of you came by and closed that door. I suppose ain't nothing unusual been happening around here in a long time."

Jones looked at Terri, and then back to Glover, "Why do you think we are driving around checking you out?"

"I saw one of you boys out here last week, and the week before, and before that," Glover described what he believed to be an unmarked patrol car cruising the neighborhood.

Terri and Jones knew that other than the false alarm, they had not been to the residence.

"Let's go in!" Jones was eager to push in a door and do an armed residential sweep. His military experiences were kicking in.

"Wait, just wait. We need more than an open garage door. It isn't even open now. I have an idea though, hold on," she turned back to Glover.

"Do you have a key for the residence, Mr. Glover?" Terri asked, recalling how her neighbor, Mrs. Casey had a key to her house just in case she locked herself out.

"I don't really know the folks. They come and go and mostly go. Florida I think, snowbirds you call 'em. Can't stand the chilly air and go for the winter," Glover filled them in on the habits of the residents.

"Do you know their names or have a phone number for them, you know just in case you had to call them because their house was on fire?" Terri thought he was lying to her. He seemed the type of guy that would let himself in and snoop around when they aren't home.

"No, but I think Deanna does," he ignored her comment and pointed across the street to 51179 Monica.

An older woman was leaning against her little

white picket fence, watching the commotion. The side garage door being left unlocked, probably a fluke. Terri reasoned.

She spoke with Jones and Pierce about the next option in their investigation, "No answer and no signs of entry. What do you guys think? I can walk the dog around the house, but it won't do a bit of good if we are just walking around houses and don't know what we are looking for," Terri stated.

"I smell a hiding rat. Why don't we kick the door in – you know – exigent circumstances? Maybe somebody in there needs our help?"

"Jarhead! That military mindset will get us fired if not killed!" Pierce was quick to respond.

"Okay then, why don't we do it your way and just get a search warrant and see what is in there?" Jones was a bit naive about what was necessary to obtain one. Or maybe his prior experience had allowed a bit more leniency when it came to judiciary discretion.

"Randy, uh, based on what? Because you believe someone should answer the door? There is no probable cause. Let's see what Deanna has to say, and then we will clear out of here," Terri decided.

"Hopefully she has the phone number for the home owners and possibly a key," Terri told them.

She walked across the street to speak with Deanna, "Deanna?" She asked a woman in her mid-70's already standing near the gate.

"Yes. Is everything ok?" Deanna asked since there were two patrol units parked in front of her address and the nosy neighbor Glover was outside talking to the police.

This will be interesting, let's see who knows more about the neighborhood – nosy old coot or crotchety woman, Jones thought.

"Have you seen anything or anyone next door?" Terri began what she hoped would be a short interview.

"No, nothing, not even a car. But I did notice that the garage door had been open a couple of days ago. I

79

was going to call, but I thought that stuffy old man called you guys because today the door was closed," Deanna's eyes squinted toward Glover.

"When did you first notice the side door open, ma'am?" Terri asked.

"Well, it was maybe two days ago. Maybe it was one time last week, I can't remember when. But you can see it isn't open today. I thought one of you guys came by and closed it," Deanna stated the obvious.

"Why would you think it was one of us? Did you see a patrol car?" Terri asked.

"No, I didn't, but I don't know who else would have closed it."

"Do you know who lives there?" Terri continued the inquisition.

"Sure do. Been neighbors our whole lives. Barb and Mark Donnelly. Nicest people. They are in Florida for a bit. Went to see their son. They have two sons, and they head off every couple of months to stay with one of them. Their one boy, Jacob, he married his high school sweetheart, and they moved to Coral Falls last year," Deanna began a rambling tangent.

Terri interrupted, "Would you happen to have their phone number?"

"Of course, dear. I have the phone numbers of most of my neighbors, even nosy John. Although I never call him but I bet he sure would like me to call him," Deanna began again.

"Can you call them for me please?" Terri asked.

"Oh, sure. I'll call them right now. I hope I don't catch Barb out by the pool. She loved the sun, and last year when they came back she was so tan, why you would have thought..." Deanna is again interrupted as Barb Donnelly answered.

"Barb? How are you? How is the weather? Really? Is that right?" Deanna started a conversation Terri knew would not be short.

"May I speak to her please?" Terri interjected.

"Just a second Barb, the police want to talk to

you. No, no, well he isn't here, it is that female one. Bradford, yeah ok, hold on," Deanna handed the phone to Terri.

"Mrs. Donnelly? This is Detective Terri Bradford with the Waterford Police Department. I have a couple of questions if you aren't too busy," Terri waited for a response. After receiving the go-ahead, she continued, "I understand you and your husband are out of town for an extended period? Yes, well how long have you been gone?"

Barb told her they had been gone about two months and were visiting her son and his wife in Florida for another week or so. They then planned on returning home.

"Does anyone else live in your house? A renter, perhaps?" Terri questioned about other possible persons with access.

"How long have you lived at the address?" Terri had heard of the Donnelly's, the town being so small, but she didn't have a personal relationship with them. There weren't very many people she hadn't heard of in Waterford, but they had lived there for the past 20 years. She wondered how she had not known of them.

"No? Just you and your husband, I see. Yes, thank you. Well, it seems your neighbors have noticed the side garage door open. Yes, yes that is correct, sometimes the wind does push doors open. But then they say the door was closed, and as far as I know, doors may open from the wind or close from the wind, but typically they do not do both," Terri provided an unlikely probability to Barb Donnelly.

She got more to the point, "Mrs. Donnelly, your house is secure, and there are no indications that anything is amiss, but the home alarm was activated two weeks ago, and your house was found secure then. This is the second time we have been out here. Did the alarm company get a hold of you?"

"Oh, I see. The alarm company doesn't have the forwarding number. If it is all right with you, we would like to check the inside of your residence just to ensure nothing is out of order," Terri asked for consent to complete a cursory search of the interior of the home.

"Yes, yes ma'am. Does Deanna have a key? Okay, great. I will have her let us in then, and we will call you back shortly. It may take about 20 minutes, ma'am. Of course, yes, certainly we will call you and let you know," Terri hung up with Barb Donnelly and turned to Deanna.

"Would you please grab the key to their house, ma'am? We are just going to check it out and make sure nothing is out of place," Terri explained she had gotten verbal consent from Barb to enter the house.

"Just a minute, I'll get the key and slip my shoes on," Deanna closed the door as Terri waited on the porch. When she appeared, they walked across the street together.

"That's how you get things done, Jarhead, take notes," Pierce poked him in the side as they walked to the house. Terri waited for Deanna.

Jones was leaning against his squad car flipping through papers. Pierce was still conversing with the neighbor; he was pacing back and forth, literally wearing a two-foot path in the grass by the time Terri and Deanna walked back across the street.

Entering the garage, Deanna was hesitant to give the key to Terri and insisted on unlocking the door so she could hold onto it.

"There you go, dear," she pushed the inside garage door open.

"Step back, please ma'am. It's best if you wait here in the garage."

Jones walked in behind, "Ma'am, please go back outside and wait. There is no need for you to be standing in here," he repeated. She ignored the request and stood near the side door.

"I'm not going to ask you again, ma'am. Please move outside; preferably back to your house. Officer Bradford will return the key when we are done," Jones shifted into military drill-sergeant mode.

"Waterford Police! Anyone here?" Terri called into the house, her voice echoed in the emptiness. She drew her service weapon and entered the foyer from the garage. There were no shoes in the hall to trip on, and she noticed the bathroom to the left. *Empty.*

Jones was right behind Terri as they entered the kitchen. Nothing seemed out of place, no dishes in the sink, the chairs are leveled to the table. Another foyer off the end of the kitchen, but it had opened up into a living room.

They decided to investigate the living room first. Terri noticed the yellow light on the DSL box was on, but the television was off. *A power surge probably explains the false alarm*, she thought. They entered the hall off the living room, Terri and Jones cleared two bedrooms and the master bath as well.

Retreating to the living room, they saw no entryway for a basement, so they continued back through the kitchen and cautiously entered the family room.

Standing in disbelief, she saw a crumpled person upon the floor. *He was wearing brown shoes, blue jeans, and a blue button-up dress shirt, dark hair.* He was face down. She scanned the room for potential threats.

After finding nothing, she approached the body. Her heart was in her throat, and for a moment, she didn't breathe at all, "Check the last door and the closet," she nervously barked an order to Jones who was standing beside her, his eyes frozen to the mass of a man. He was more surprised than she.

"Jones – do it!" She ordered again.

"Locked, Terri," Jones checked the back door, "Clear. All Clear – we're good."

Oh shit! Terri examined the body stretched out on the floor. *Left, right, up, down.* Terri kneeled to check for a pulse, but the body was clearly in a state of rigor, and her effort was pointless. *Nothing. No movement, nothing.* "Oh my God, he is dead. Is this the guy that came in to register?"

Jones was already talking over her, "Holy shit. That's George Moore. That's the offender that came in and tried to verify his address. Maybe that bastard was telling the truth!"

"We better call Captain Williams. She is not going to like this. Get some tape out there and rope off the driveway."

Jones exited the house, picked up Deanna along the way; she was still standing in the garage. "Ma'am, I told you to go home. I will arrest you for obstruction, don't test me," he barked.

After having to escort her all the way home, Jones turned to Pierce and said slow and softly, "Pierce, we got a cold one in there. Let's get this place roped off."

"What?" Pierce asked in disbelief.

"There's a stiff in there; he's dead. And it's George Moore. Probably been dead a day or two, or more, maybe less. I have no clue. I don't smell anything yet, but he is good and dead. Terri wants you to call the Captain and let her know. In the meantime, I am going to run back to the station and grab the crime scene kit and your camera. Need anything else?" Jones acted like it was already old news.

Pierce was standing with his jaw dropped, "What?" he repeated. "Another one?"

"Yes, another dead guy. He is in there on the floor," Jones repeated.

"Wait, what? Somebody else is dead? Moore? Are you sure? How? Wait, I have to go see this," Pierce walked by Jones and headed through the house to the back room.

"It is the guy I told to come back to the station with his correct address the other day," Jones followed him inside.

"Whoa...it sure is another one. He should have taken your advice Jarhead, and changed his damn address," Pierce stated flatly.

Terri looked up, "Yes. Unbelievable. As soon as you get pictures, we can flip him and look for identification. Or wait. That could be a wallet," Terri pointed to the square impression in his back pocket.

"Yep. I'm sure you're right. It looks like a wallet. Want me to grab it? He does look like the guy from your list, that Moore fella," Pierce reached down to remove it.

"Stop! Not without gloves, you don't," she reminded him of the possible forensic evidence.

"Gotcha, be right back," Pierce didn't have gloves with him.

"I've got some. You could just take my gloves, and if you tell me where the camera is, I will run back to the station and grab it," Jones offered.

Pierce thought about it for a few seconds. Let Jones touch my camera or put my hands inside Jones's gloves. Jones could see the sweat bead up on his forehead.

"Give me a minute; I will go and get it. The camera, and where are your gloves? Put them on already and see if this poor sap has some identification," his decision was made.

"Alright Terri, are we taking bets on this guys' name?" Jones was always willing to make wagers he could win.

Terri was leaning over the victim without touching him. She was examining a broken pool cue, which was the probable murder weapon. She looked for the other half, but he had probably fallen on it. There was a definite indentation on the right side of this man's face, and she began to feel like this was no accident.

"I will take that to mean you already owe me a beer and you don't want to buy me another one, since you did not answer," Jones carefully pulled the wallet from the deceased back pocket. It was brown leather and contained a couple of credit cards, a driver license, business cards, and $45.00.

"George Ronald Moore," Jones read aloud.

"This is absolutely the guy that said he lived here. And absolutely the guy that came in the other day. He was a flaming asshole," he repeated the name so Terri could write it down before returning the wallet to the pocket.

"George Moore was obviously someone the Donnelly's did not know," Terri stated, "Now, about that camera?"

"Pierce already left to go get it. And the crime scene and evidence tech kits, too. I should have told him to bring us back a coke," he realized he was growing thirsty.

"What's this?" Jones was looking at a Waterford Police Department business card. Officer David Cooper, SOR was scrawled on the back.

"What does it say?" Terri asked.

"Looks like a business card from the office, Coop must have registered him last time. It has yesterdays date on it, and that's when he came in," Jones laid it out on the pool table near the wallet and other items so Pierce would remember to photograph the contents.

"Let's get started. You can start sketching out the scene. I'll get the medical examiner on the phone. After that, I will call Mike and have him bring us a couple of cokes on the way back," she smiled.

Jones had the scene sketched in minutes and was chomping at the bit to do something else while they waited.

"C'mon Randy, let's take some notes," Terri was already looking around.

They started back at the garage and tried to walk the same path. There were a couple of newspapers lying at the garage door, inside. *That's weird why would there be newspapers if they were out of town?* Terri wondered.

"Randy, did you see any mail? I don't see any, so why would there be two newspapers left here by the door. Can you see the date on them without touching them?" Terri asked.

"Yeah, one is last Saturday, and the other is Saturday before. We will collect those and send them for prints – just in case," he was going to find something that would break the case wide open.

"Do you see anything that could have been used to get the inside door open?" They scoured the garage and interior hallway for something that might pick a lock.

"What's this?" Jones spotted a silver blade with a sharp point.

"Letter opener I believe. It has the initials 'CMT' on the handle. Is that some kind of brand?" He asked.

"I have no idea. Is that blood on the handle?" She saw a pinkish smattering that appeared to be blood.

"I'm not sure, either way, I'm going to have Pierce photograph it, and we can send it to the lab. It seems out of place to me."

They documented the item, and the location then stepped around it and into the kitchen. They walked through each room a little bit, but they were careful not to touch anything.

"Something is not right here," Terri stated. "Some things are missing. Like I don't see this guy in any pictures. I don't see his name anywhere. I don't see shoes that would fit him by the door. Let me check something," she opened the refrigerator door and stood there analyzing the contents.

This refrigerator is practically empty. Bottled water, ketchup, mustard, mayonnaise, cans of coke pushed to the back, "He doesn't stay her Randy. We need to see if he has a room here. We need to verify if he has a bed, or clothes, or anything personal."

"Terri, do you think he was killed here? Or brought here after?" He was staring at the body.

"I don't know. But I don't think you could carry that man in here. If it was someplace else, then there must have been more than one person dumping him off," she stated.

"I don't understand why the man would be registering his sex offender address here if he doesn't live here."

"I can't find any evidence that he has ever lived here. Can you?" Honestly, not unless he and the old man share slippers in the wife's bedroom, I am going to agree with..." Terri cut him off.

"It looks like he should have taken your advice," her voice trailed off as she stood to consider what his death might mean.

"When Pierce comes back, we need to dust these light switches for prints," she said to Jones.

"I'm going to see if he can do these floors, too. We have our shoes, but I think he may be able to get the victim's and maybe the suspect's impressions as well," Jones knew footwear impressions could be hiding on the highly polished and clean wood floors, and they could be just as incrementing as latent fingerprints.

The bottom of each shoe has a specific size, tread, and wear patterns; even the scratches and scuffmarks on the shoes are unique and could be matched to the suspect's shoes.

She left Jones to look around while she walked out to the backyard to call Ryann, "Honey, I'm afraid I am going to be a little bit late tonight," Terri said into the phone.

"Again? Really?" Ryann whined but caught herself before complaining.

"Well, this time it's a big deal. I can't talk about it right now," Terri was irritated, I shouldn't have to explain anyway.

"Promise you will tell me all about it when you have a chance?" Ryann was sincere.

"I will be at home if you want to call later when you are done," Terri gave a half-ass attempt at reassuring her, distracted entirely by what was shaping up to be not just another murder, but maybe a serial killer on the loose.

"I will call you when I get home," she repeated.

Chapter 8

Terri was hoping Bob's would be empty; it was only 9 pm and a little early for the regular crowd. She knew Trisha would be working and needed to chitchat with her friend to relieve a little stress.

She rolled into the drive to find three or four other vehicles in the lot. She recognized Trish's car and parked next to it. She always bounced her troubles off of her best friend, and she thought she might even drink a beer or two then head home. Tomorrow would be another long and busy day, but after what she had witnessed this afternoon, she was ready for a drink.

"Hey Trish," Terri said half-heartedly, "Give me a Captain and diet."

"Depends, my friend. Are you on duty or off duty?" Trisha was almost always the voice of reason.

Terri didn't respond.

"Got it," Trisha said. "How about a diet minus the Captain? It's not 11 yet unless you are out early and off duty my friend." She served the icy coke in a chilled glass before Terri even sat down.

"Long day?" Trisha asked, "You are right. I have Duke in the car anyway. Long day, well, kind of, I..." her comment interrupted by the crash of cymbals.

"Hello, this is Terri," she answered rather flatly. Nothing, "Hello? Say something, damn it!" She closed the phone and slammed it down on the bar top, "Damn telemarketers! How the hell did they get my number in the first place?" Terri cursed.

"No one important I assume?" Trisha asked, not hearing her remark about the telemarketers. "You are here early, and you have that look on your face. What's going on?" Trisha knew her and she recognized something wasn't quite right.

"Another one Trish. Another one," she said.

"What? You guys found another box?" Trisha's voice dropped to a husky whisper as she tossed out the far-fetched idea.

"Shhhhh. Yes. Well, no. Not a box, a dead guy," she said softly.

Trish nearly dropped the glass she was holding, "What? Who?" Where? Out on Stern Creek Road?"

"I can't talk about it right now. I'm seriously ready to go home, but I'm sure I won't be able to sleep. I am sure there is something I should be doing right now to solve that murder, too. I'm tired. I will be off tomorrow afternoon, at least I should be, and we can talk about it when I have more time."

She didn't really want to talk about it, but she tried to keep her best friend in the loop. That's part of the reason they were so close, she trusted her. Trisha, to her credit, never spoke about the stories Terri confided to her.

"Terri, you guys got another murder?" Trish wanted to know.

"Yes, but not in a box, and not on Stern Creek Road. I can't talk about it right now," Terri wasn't ready to divulge any information.

Terri gulped the first drink and tuned into the evening news flashing above on the back bar flat screen. *Nothing yet, thankfully,* she saw the weather pop up and the alert screen at the bottom had no mention of the latest crime.

She spun around on the bar stool as Trisha refilled the beverage and placed the popcorn within arms reach.

Her eyes scanned the room to see what locals made their way to the bar and she saw the town drunk, Bart Nelson propped against the jukebox. She could barely hear the song but knew it would probably be some old country tune by Conway Twitty or Loretta Lynn. Bart was always in a solemn mood.

His wife died in a car crash about ten years ago. He still hadn't gotten over it and continued to blame the County for not keeping the road up. To think of it, that was the first time Stern Creek Road had taken lives. David's wife and daughter were the second and third.

Her eyes were starting to glaze from the dark fluorescent-lit bar room and lack of dinner as she continued to scan the room. *Is that...no, it can't be,* Terri's skin turned prickly. *What was her name? I have her card...what was her name?* Terri twisted the chair back around trying to remember.

"You look like you just saw a ghost," Trisha commented, "You okay?"

"Yeah, see the lady sitting next to the pool table, with the guy in the red shirt?" Terri asked.

"Yes, she has been coming in here for a couple of weeks with that same fella," Trisha retorted, turning her back to Terri. She could tell that this woman sparked something in Terri, even if that was only curiosity.

"I think that's her. The woman I told you about," she tried hard not to act interested, but Trisha saw right through it.

Suddenly the woman was at Terri's back.

"Hi. Officer Bradford. Allison, Allison Ross," the woman reminded her.

"Yes, yes I remember from Stern Creek Road. I see you found the Main okay," Terri acted as if she could barely remember, for Trisha's sake.

Allison ran her hand down Terri's back. Closing her eyes, Terri imagined she was not wearing her bullet-resistant vest as she felt the pressure in her touch.

"Can I get you a drink, Miss...Miss?" Trisha was expecting to be introduced.

"Yes please, it's Coke. And could you bring it to our table?" Allison instructed, obviously not wanting Trisha involved in the private conversation.

Not much in the mood to argue, Terri left the bar stool and followed Allison to her table. Terri saw that Allison was wearing another short maroon colored skirt. It was just as long as the one she was wearing the first time they met. *Look at those legs; Tina would be jealous,* Terri thought as a vivid image of Tina Turner in fishnet stockings flashed into her mind.

Before they reached the table, Allison lifted her arm and waved her wrist. A thick silver bangle caught the table candle and flashed a bright glow off of her matching pendant necklace. She adjusted both before returning to her seat. Instantly the man got up from the table and left the bar.

"Who was that?" Terri asked. She was impressed with the power she held by merely flicking her wrist.

"He is a friend of mine, Alex," Allison offered, and pulled out a chair, "Sit."

Terri sat without thinking, "What brings you to Bob's?" she asked not really wanting to know. She was thankful for the distraction, though. Her eyes weighed heavily on the silky cream camisole. Her breasts, all showing but the nipple, were perked invitingly upward.

"I'm glad I ran into you. I've been doing a little research, and I think I might need your help. Are you familiar with the cemetery off Stern Creek?" Allison looked down as she spoke.

Trisha dropped the drinks off and stood around for payment.

"Trish, I'll take care of it in a minute," Terri said wanting her to leave so they could talk.

"I thought maybe we could meet there; I don't like your friends nosing around my business," Allison gave a glance to Trisha.

Terri looked at Trisha, "Trisha? She is harmless, and she seriously doesn't give a shit about police work."

Trisha returned the look and mouthed, "Is everything okay?"

Terri shook her head yes, and Trisha walked away knowing she would call her if needed.

"What do you have here?" Terri asked about a couple of folders on the table. They had a casual conversation about some traffic crash investigations Allison had completed, and Allison began asking some questions about Stern Creek Road when Terri's phone rang again.

She looked at the name, Ryann. She didn't answer; instead, she turned to Allison and told her she had to head home.

"No problem, I have to head out also," Allison grabbed her purse and stood up. Terri continued to stare at her chest and found herself slightly embarrassed when their eyes met.

Terri found herself silent and captivated, and she again followed Allison toward the door. Catching herself more interested in answering a question from the first time she saw her about the lace panties.

Terri turned and shouted to Trisha, "I'll catch up to you in a little bit."

They stepped out of the bar as the thunder cracked against the sky. Allison jumped and grabbed onto Terri's arm, "I'm sorry," she said, her voice a little shaky, "That startled me."

They walked a short distance across the parking lot and Terri noticed she hadn't let go of her arm yet, which was okay with her. Allison led her to a Ford Expedition.

This is a different vehicle than I remember, Terri thought. Allison noticed her looking and immediately told her it was a rental, "I don't like putting miles on my car," she explained.

The wind was starting to pick up as Terri opened the door for her, "Meet me at the cemetery?" Allison asked again.

Terri helped her climb into the four-wheel drive and commented, "Well, I didn't expect to see you, and tonight I have a previous commitment."

"I would like to see you, when you have time. Hopefully soon?" Allison asked.

"It must be important if you are tracking me down, or maybe you just wanted to see me?" She smiled and leaned toward her.

Allison held the folder and patted it twice as she sat it down on the passenger seat, "Strictly business this time," she said.

Terri was disappointed; "Perhaps we can talk about it over lunch?"

Allison closed the door and rolled the window down, "Of course, I would love to see you." She started the vehicle and drove off.

Terri stood flatfooted – "Uh, where did your friend go?" She asked into the wind as she watched the taillights escape from view.

Terri walked back to the bar and made good on the bill. She would catch up with Trisha tomorrow and fill her in.

"Don't forget about Ryann," Trisha reminded her.

Cymbals clashed repeatedly, and Terri flipped open the phone, "Hello?" she mumbled into the receiver. Her phone had been ringing nearly 10 minutes, and she had finally heard it. By the time she answered the caller had hung up, but it was another blocked call. She didn't give it another thought and headed out to the car and then home.

Cymbals clanged again, and Terri snagged her cell phone from her pocket. *I hope this isn't Randy…oh God…*Her stomach dropped as she answered the phone. She always feared she would cut out early, leaving her partner to finish picking up the pieces of a simple case and something tragic would happen.

"Hello, this is Terri," she said as professionally as possible, glad she hadn't eaten anything yet as it might come right back up.

"Hello, this is Terri," she repeated into the phone. *No answer. Someone is breathing into the phone*, she thought. She checked the cell phone face; the time was running.

"Hello," Terri closed the phone and hit the incoming call list. *Unknown caller. Third time tonight.* She dialed star 69 and hoped the number would pop up.

"The number you are trying to reach is unavailable," the automated voice on the other end said as she fired up the patrol car.

Suddenly the dispatcher's voice broke the silence, "3742, are you still available to take a 15 complaint on Stern Creek Road?" the radio bellowed.

Terri snapped up the in-car prep radio and blurted, "'I'm not too far from there now, and it is on my way to out of service. What do you have?" She knew a code '15' was a suspicious situation.

"3742, this is the third call tonight. Could you check a suspicious vehicle? It is a dark colored 2-door vehicle with window tint, unknown plate, and unknown number of occupants. It has been driving the blocks at Stern Creek for some time. Do you want another unit?" Dispatch sounded concern.

That's just dispatch overreacting. He is so protective of me, and he knows I have my boy. Terri thought, she turned to look back at Duke, panting, sprawled across the back seat as if he had a stressful day. "Nah, I'll check it out and advise," she responded and stepped on the accelerator.

"2231," the dispatcher shot back the time.

"Is there a complainant that wants to be seen?" She inquired.

"No complainant. The calls are coming from a cell phone. Let me know if you need another. 2232," Dispatch again with the time.

Terri made her way from Main to Stern Creek Road. She rounded the bend and saw nothing. *No headlights, no tail lights. This is a desolate road. No one traveled this way. As a matter of fact, there are only two houses on this stretch of road. Who would be out here to even call this in? Maybe it is our killer,* she was imagining running directly into the killer, leaving a box in the field and she would be there to arrest him singlehandedly.

"3742, dispatch- put me in the area, so far UTL," Terri let him know she was okay and there really was nothing out there. She drove a small stretch shining the patrol vehicle spotlight up and down the fields. There weren't any tracks leading off the road and no other evidence that someone else might be there.

"I have you in the area 3742, 2336," Dispatch still sounded concerned.

"Let me check the rest of the road. So far, we're good up to the u-bend," Terri described the U-turn type curve in the road that could be mistaken for a dead-end. The fact was, the road followed Stern Creek, and it had many twists and turns.

"You are set to go 1030 when you clear," Dispatch stated, giving her the out of service code.

She had been working with him for several years now and felt like he was one of her better friends, sometimes a little too protective, but Anthony was Anthony.

Terri arrived at the U-turn; her spotlight caught a glimmer of something in the thickets. She drove a little closer toward the reflection. *Taillight reflectors.* "3742," Terri said again into the prep.

"3742 go ahead," Dispatch answered promptly.

"I've got a couple of taillights off of the road down near the creek. Could you start me another unit for backup? It looks like a vehicle run off the road at the curve. Just give me an ETA," she asked for an estimated time of arrival on the other unit.

"3721, show me on the way to back 3742," Officer Ed Reese responded to the request for backup. He was the night patrol, which he mostly spent at the all-night diner drinking coffee.

Reese was an ole' coot who had been on the force since 1979, he should have retired, but he just wouldn't. At least he was willing to hang out and collect overtime when everyone else was ready to go home, and tonight, she was glad he was around.

While she waited for back up, Terri got Duke out of the car and let him stretch. It would be at least 15 minutes before Reese could get there. She enjoyed seeing her dog work, he was eager to please and was pacing back and forth. The field probably reminded him of training exercises at the training center.

"Might as well start a wrecker while we wait," she

requested of Dispatch.

"It's already on the way," Anthony was efficient like that.

"Hey Terri, watcha got?" Reese rolled his window down as he pulled up and stopped.

"Hi, Ed. There is a vehicle in the field. A Jeep, I think," Terri shined her flashlight in the direction of the tail light reflectors. Her spotlight was already fixed upon the rear of the vehicle.

"Looks like someone drove it in sideways, tried to straighten it out, and the front wheels must have landed in Stern Creek," Terri told him.

During the heavy rains, the creek was usually three feet higher. It would not have made a difference though, either the engine would be flooded or the front end would be caught on the rocks.

"Yep, sure does. Let's go have a look," he put his vehicle in park and got out.

Reese began walking toward the vehicle, "Probably dumped the front end in the creek and put the frame on the drop," he was guessing, but he was right.

Terri and Duke set out with him. Approaching the scene cautiously they surveyed the vehicle; it was empty. She gave the registration plate information to dispatch and had Anthony run a query on it.

He was back with a quick response, "3742, your status on the vehicle," he was prepared to air the inquiry on the vehicle.

"Go ahead," they were expecting to hear the name of the owner and a local address.

"Your registration plate, 'one-one-two-seven, j-john, j-john, f-frank, returns on a Jeep Wrangler to Airport Rentals, Limited out of New York. It's a rental vehicle with no other information. Go ahead."

Dispatch grew more curious and wanted to ask a couple of questions, but he knew he could call Terri on her cell phone and get the rental information if she decided to give it to him.

"Can you enter it into the system as abandoned

and towed? I'll see if I can't get you the rental information so we can call them," Terri knew the rental papers would have the address of the company, along with a phone number. Usually, the name of the renter would be on the forms as well, including the rental return date.

"Terri, did you see this?" Reese was standing on the road in front of his patrol vehicle. The road was torn up with circular tire tracks, "Looks like some kids out here doing donuts on the road."

"It sure does, and it kind of looks like there is more than one set of vehicle tracks headed into the weeds," she fixed her spotlight on a set of tracks leading to the Jeep, and another set of tracks about twenty yards away. A third set of tracks made a wide continuous turn and exited after the corner of the road. The tracks into the field were evident from the bent over thickets.

"There is another set over there. Odd, don't you think? It gives me the impression that someone intentionally drove this vehicle into the creek. Not once, but several times," Terri observed.

"Damn kids. Just out having a good old time. Until the truck got stuck," Reese reflected on his days of youthful stupidity.

"You all set out there?" Dispatch was asking.

"Yeah, the wrecker is rolling up to the scene. 3721 and I are going to wait with it," she told him. She let Duke run a little on his leash while she inspected the dirt tracks. They were in a circular fashion like she had thought, but it was impossible to tell what type of vehicle it was that made the tracks, but she was reasonably sure it was the Jeep in the Creek.

The wrecker driver drove most of the way to the Jeep and stopped about ten yards short. He pulled the rigging winch to the rear tow clip of the 4 x 4 and hooked on. The vehicle was out of the trench in no time. Since the keys were left in the ignition, Reese got in and drove it to the road to make it easier on the wrecker driver to load.

"Terri, would you mind searching it and getting me the vehicle identification number and I will get a complaint number?" he wasn't wearing his glasses and Terri happily obliged.

"No problem, 'Stay,'" she ordered Duke to sit at the front of the vehicle while she searched for the rental paperwork. *None. Hmmm.* She checked the inside of the door and wrote the VIN in her pocket notebook.

"No paperwork, Ed," she yelled.

"Maybe the rental company can tell us who rented it," Reese was angling to write a citation for leaving the scene of an accident or at the very least, failing to report one.

"I'll let the rental company know we have the Jeep. No holds on it, though. Whoever rented it will have to pay for the wrecker and any damage, but that will be their problem," Terri told him.

Reese scratched the complaint number on a business card and told the wrecker driver to hook it up and release it to the rental company.

"Do you want me to call them?" He asked.

"If you don't mind. Maybe I should call them tonight though, find out who rented it. Maybe they don't know it's out here."

"Look, Terri. There isn't anybody complaining, and the Jeep hasn't been reported to be stolen, what is there to investigate?" He made a good point.

"Yeah, I know. Then I guess you don't need anything from me," Terri was disappointed, but she knew he was right. If there was no complainant and no crime, then why waste time.

"I'm good. See you in a few days. I'm off the rest of the weekend," Reese turned his spotlight to better highlight the Jeep, now that the wrecker driver had moved it.

"Oh and Terri, I will get the info from the rental company for you and leave it on your desk."

"Thanks, Ed. Have a good weekend," Terri snapped her fingers and pointed toward her Tahoe. Duke obeyed and waited for her to open his door. Tired, she called out of service and finally headed toward home.

Chapter 9

"Terri, it's Randy, you okay? I didn't get any sleep. Have you slept?" Jones asked.

"What time is it? Did I oversleep? I must have overslept and the phone woke me up. I'm sorry Randy. What's going on?" Terri sounded half apologetic. She looked at the clock, *nine thirty, shit.*

"Good news, first. Cooper said he would pick up the autopsy report on Moore today at the medical examiner's office," Jones sounded more excited than he eluded.

"Seriously, Randy? You called me to tell me David was going to actually do some work?" Terri asked.

"No, Terri. You were supposed to be here at 9, remember?"

Terri breathed heavily into the phone, still trying to exhale the fatigue from her body, "I'm sorry, Randy."

"Coop should be back by the time you come in, and we've got the autopsy report from the 'Box Guy.' The medical examiner's currier dropped off the sealed report at 9. I can't wait for you to get here so we can go over it!" Jones sounded excited, and he knew better than to open Terri's mail, but he was hoping she would make an exception in this case.

"Great! Give me about thirty minutes. You guys have coffee made already? I'm definitely going to need some."

Damn it, Terri, you can't let me open this fucking envelope? Randy composed himself, "Sure, Terri. See you then," his disappointment evident in his voice.

A little more up-beat now, Terri didn't even think about calling Ryann. Instead, she called Trisha. "Trish, can you watch Duke while I run into work? A few things came up, and I need you to keep him. I can pick him up later tonight or tomorrow, so I will drop him off in about 15 minutes," Terri blurted, not giving her a chance to decline or ask any more questions about the encounter with

Allison.

Driving in, Terri tried to focus on work, but her mind was pre-occupied. She was still wondering what Allison had wanted, and again, she had forgotten to call Ryann.

Two quick blasts of cymbals, Terri's phone was ringing. *Ryann. Shit, if I don't answer she'll think something's wrong if I do answer...shit...* "Hey, Babe! I'm so sorry for not getting back to you when I got in, I was just so tired," she lied as she spoke into the receiver.

She wondered how and if she was going to have to explain what really happened, not just the homicide investigation that kept her at work late but with Allison in the parking lot of the bar. *I've never had to explain myself before so why the hell should I start now?* She asked herself.

"Hi, you. I was a little worried when you didn't call me, but I figured you were busy at work and then you would be tired. Anyway, I was just thinking about you, and I thought I would call. Are we on for dinner tonight?" Ryann asked.

"I think so. I'm actually headed to work right now; it seems we just received some important information about a case we are working," Terri told her; the excitement was apparent in her voice as she turned the conversation to focus on work.

"Okay, babe. Call me when you get free. I'd like to spend some time with you. I am so ready to spend some time with you, maybe a vacation together?" Ryann asked.

"We can talk about it later, okay?" Terri told her that she had to get concentrating on work and they hung up leaving it for a different day to discuss.

"Whew," Terri breathed a sigh of relief, "I'll deal with that later," she stated out loud and leaned over to turn the radio up. She was relieved to hear the morning news gave no information about the two homicides. The public was already blowing up the phones, not to mention every newscaster in the state was begging for information.

Terri stopped at the gas station on the way in, fueled up and grabbed a Diet Coke for later. She knew the vending machine had been empty for about a month, since David was supposed to keep track of the vending orders, and no one filled in for him while he was gone. She knew it would be at least another week before David's lazy ass would get around to filling it.

Terri parked in her usual spot, then headed straight for the detective cubicles at the back, "Hey, Jack," she waved in acknowledgment as she passed him.

"Terri, the autopsy report is on your desk like you asked," Jones said happily, "and I have the photographs from Pierce to review." He had nearly met her at the door when she arrived. He handed her a large manila envelope with the words "Stern Creek Road" written across the top with the file number 029-612-06.

"Also, Reese dropped some information for you on that rental vehicle, which is on your desk, too."

"Guess what else we have from the State Lab?" Jones grinned ear to ear, "the Fingerprint Analysis confirming George Moore as our second victim," Jones blurted before she could offer an answer.

"Seriously? Already? Those guys in the forensic laboratory are amazingly fast, especially with prints for direct comparison," Terri was impressed. "I didn't see David, I thought you told me he was picking up the report?"

"Coop was supposed to pick the report up, but he called right after I got off the phone with you, he said he couldn't pick it up right away, and that something came up. I called the lab, and they actually faxed the front page to me," Jones liked to get things done.

She looked at it for a moment then placed it on her desk next to the coroner report, "I could use that coffee now."

Jones produced one seemingly out of thin air, "I knew you would need this." He set it down on the desk as she hung her jacket on the back of the door.

She took a deep breath, "Well, John Doe, let's see who you really are and what killed you," she sat down to open the laboratory report.

She opened the forensic envelope with a double edge switchblade she had confiscated from a couple of high school kids. Jones stood near her listening intently as she read, "An AFIS scan of the fingerprints have produced the following results: When entered into the database, a search concluded nearly 20 latent prints suitable for comparison analysis," Terri frowned and continued to read.

"Further analysis and comparison determined the submitted prints to be those of the first returning selection: Kevin William Kramer, Caucasian male, 05-11-1984."

Terri scanned down the page and began reading the legal jargon from the Latent Print Unit at the Laboratory when Jones interrupted.

"What? Holy Shit, Terri, both of these guys were on my hunt list. Pierce and I, I mean, I just put together two files on guys we were going to hunt down. Kramer is the first guy, and Moore is the second guy, and then there is one more," Jones hesitated to tell her about Hines, but it was probably time to reveal his secret investigation.

"Let me see the files on these guys, where have they been registering? When did they last register and where?" She took the files and checked out their cover sheets. The third paper was only a name and birthday, Jeremy Hines, August 18, 1981. It was scratched on the center of the page.

"Get a run on this guy, also, and find out where he lived. Don't forget his criminal history," Terri ordered.

"On it," Jones had already logged into his computer and was pulling up the law enforcement information interface.

Terri flipped through the autopsy report for the CAUSE OF DEATH heading; she found it on the last page, under 'Opinion.'

"The Waterford County Medical Examiner, Alexa

Anderson, D.O., has performed an autopsy on the body of Kevin Kramer at the request of the Waterford Police Department and found the cause of death to be: asphyxia, secondary to laryngeal trauma, secondary to blunt force trauma to the neck."

She continued reading, "The absence of petechial hemorrhages in the eyes, face, lungs, and neck area further discount the probability of strangulation, however, the cause of death has been determined to be asphyxia due to fracture of the hyoid bones and larynx."

Terri gave a sigh as she set the report down, and she sipped her coffee, "Where is David? I want to see how Moore was killed."

"Serial killer, Terri? You think?" Jones speculated.

"Wait. What is this?" Terri asked Jones of the large envelope that had been pushed to the corner of her desk.

"That's the information on the rental vehicle from Reese. He said he dropped it off for you," Jones reminded her.

"It is an express response from New York, it's sealed, or I already would have looked," he said with a smile. "I think that is the home office of the rental company, he must have gotten them to send the renter information overnight," he was waiting for her to open it.

Terri placed her coffee on the desk and started to open the envelope. Before she had a chance to rip the seal, Cooper walked in.

"Any clues yet?" He interrupted, as he helped himself to the chair in front of her desk.

"Did you get the report on Moore?" Terri asked, trying not to sound demanding; she dropped the envelope among other mail that cluttered her desk.

"Haven't had a chance to talk with you since you've been back. Did you have a nice time? What did you guys do? You have been gone a couple of weeks," Terri was trying to get a conversation going.

"Not really a vacation. I've been tying up some

loose ends and well, let's just say it was no picnic," he never talked about his personal life.

Maybe he has a new woman; maybe he met her in his 'gamer' club, Terri thought.

Cooper looked about, clearly bothered. He handed the large sealed forensic envelope to Terri, "Seems someone couldn't wait for the name. The lab told me they faxed the cover sheet already. Jones, what's the problem? You didn't think I could handle it?" Cooper shot him a look.

Terri immediately opened it to search for the cause of death.

"Anyway, I worked on my car a little, a little on the house. How come you guys didn't call me when this went out?" Cooper felt he should have been called, even though he was on vacation.

"We didn't want to bother you. Besides, you were out of town, weren't you?" Terri redirected Cooper's attention.

"Is that the other case?" He asked, carefully watching her. He seemed to be hyper-suspicious of everyone, even fellow officers.

"Randy said he tried to call you several times, but you didn't answer. He drove by your house later that night, but you must have been still out of town. And David, it has been in the newspapers and all the local buzz on television," Terri was almost interrogating him.

"Terri, come on. You know when I am on vacation, I come and go, and there isn't a television on the agenda," Cooper offered an excuse.

Terri knew he had a passion for cars and he was working on something special that he was keeping a secret. Cooper always kept secrets, especially about his cars and his gamer club.

Waterford County hosts an annual Dream Cruise event for classic and custom vehicles every fall, and he was bound and determined to get in on the winnings this year. Come to think of it she had not seen any of his vehicles, only the one that he kept in the garage. Even that one was so far from being completed it would take another five years to get in show condition.

The running office joke was that he secretly had cats and was too ashamed to let anyone know. *Probably in the garage with that car,* Terri assumed about the cats.

Cooper ignored the statement about not being home and asked, "Whatever. Tell me about the case, where are you guys with it? What's next and how can I help?"

"The lab came up with a name thanks to DNA and AFIS. Kevin Kramer," Terri offered, "Jones is doing a work-up on the guy's history. To be honest, he is a registered sex offender. The other guy is also a registered sex offender."

Cooper looked at Terri wide-eyed, "Kramer?" he said then pulled open his desk drawer realizing he may have alerted her, Terri sensed a profound personal strike and questioned, "I've never heard of either of them, have you?"

"No, no I haven't. Should I?" Cooper glared, practically shouting at her.

"David, don't be an ass. I mean they don't seem to be anyone from around here. I'm just asking if you recognized the names, not if they were your friends." Terri recomposed herself and asked him again.

He picked up an antique ceramic Precious Moments rabbit he had sitting near a picture frame of his wife and daughter. She thought it had belonged to Hayley. It was cute with ballet shoes and a soft look. Terri noticed that he sometimes picked that up when he was stressed, out of habit. He had worn the purple paint of the rabbit's hat.

"Well, I don't. Why would I?" He straightened the photo on his desk and replaced the keepsake. He excused himself to the break room for a cup of coffee.

"What's eating him?" Jones sensed the tension.

"No clue," she was still holding the medical examiner report.

"George Moore. At least we got this one right,"

she said for Jones's sake, "Cause of Death, let me see. Yes, here it is,"

Cooper spun around quickly upon hearing the next name; he had stopped right at the door.

Terri continued, "The cause of death has been determined as asphyxia due to fracture of the hyoid bones and larynx. Jesus."

"So what? Someone punched him in the throat?" Jones was immune to the violence.

"I thought you were getting coffee?" Jones asked Cooper.

"I will. Where is Pierce, isn't he in today?" Cooper walked over to his desk and began nosing around again.

Jones thought he was a little nervous, but maybe it was because he had just gotten back and the homicides bothered him.

"He had a dentist appointment and won't be in today. Randy will fill him in this afternoon and hopefully can put something together. There is obviously a consistent pattern for cause of death," Terri remarked.

There was yet another envelope to open that Pierce had left on her desk.

"Are those the photos of from the crime scene?" Cooper asked, drifting back in front of Terri.

"Yes. These are the black and white ones. I think Mike did a remarkable job," Terri surveyed the photos in order because he had photographed the scene in a clockwise pattern. They were taken before the body's position was altered or any other evidence within the scene had been manipulated.

"I'd like to see them," Cooper was reaching for them as she flipped through them.

Pierce had taken the photographs from all four corners, and it seemed nothing was missed or hidden from view by intervening objects. Pierce had paid particular attention to photographing the body and the positioning in the box. He worked his camera as a second hand and took pictures from above the victim as well.

"Jones, could you do a little work-up on this box?

I had not paid much attention to it before, but in either case, it is from somewhere. All I can make out is the last few letters, EX Industries, Meacon Bend, New York. Do you think you could find this business?" Terri shuffled more paperwork and photos across her desk.

Jones was hovering over the photos, "Of course, Terri. I will get right on it."

"Start by checking the New York small business databases to see where exactly they might be located and what they specialize in."

"I will keep looking over these photos. There must be something that we've missed," Terri placed the photographs out like a jigsaw puzzle, hoping something would stand out.

Cooper was at her back, examining the photographs. Terri could feel his breath on her hair, *gross,* she thought.

"This is not going to help," Jones said, "I'm looking at the department of licensing and regulatory affairs website for New York. They have a corporate name search. When I search for EX Industries, nearly 15000 businesses are listed."

"What do you mean, it doesn't exist?" Terri questioned.

"Well, when you enter a name in the entity corporate name search it should bring you back the name of the business so you can select it," Jones began. "Then the Articles of Corporation, Directors, and Officers of the business should be viewable, along with a business address and a mailing address. We have to narrow this list somehow."

"His employment record shows APEX Insurance; maybe the home office is out of New York?" Terri offered. She squeezed out from beneath Cooper and walked over to Jones. She watched over his shoulder as he searched the database.

"Ok, so we have this page that said 'business entity search.' So I opted to search by name, and plugged in 'Ex Industries.' Here is what popped up, a bunch of similar names, there are way too many to go over. Let's try APEX Insurance and see what comes up. We can select one, let's say, 'APEX Holdings, L.L.C.' It will tell me when it was established, what type of business it is, and it will give me addresses and phone numbers for the resident agent," Jones explained.

"In this case, the business was established in 2006 as a domestic profit corporation. The resident agent is listed as Jake Turner, but the company was automatically dissolved in 2012."

"I see. Let's try another APEX INC, by the mailing name and company name and see if that is the one we are looking for," Terri was willing to search all of the APEX names to find one out of Meacon Bend.

"Exactly. I could hand search all of these businesses, but it may take a while," Jones offered to open the electronic public filing of each business name.

"I'm not sure what we are looking for yet. I don't know if the box is even related to the crime. It is just odd that it would be postmarked from New York. I am curious about what the box originally contained. I mean, what was shipped in it and where did it ship?" Terri flooded Jones with more questions.

"That part of the box was missing, and that portion of the lid with the information was torn or cut off, wasn't it? So we are just guessing it could be APEX?"

"Yes, yes I believe it might be his employer, so maybe someone he worked with," she conjectured, "maybe we will get lucky."

"Okay, let me look through some of these," he wasted no time clicking through the names until he found one too interesting to pass up, "I think I found something."

"Lay it on me, Randy." Terri was eager to hear some good news.

"APEX INC, LLC. Doing business as APEX Insurance, Meacon Bend, New York," he read the page to Terri.

"Are you serious? What kind of insurance agency are they?" She asked.

"Life insurance, specializing in accidental death," Jones told her.

"Do you think he insured himself?" Terri smiled.

"Funny, but maybe! That's cute, but Kramer's family didn't know anything about a life insurance policy. Hell, they didn't even know he had a job!"

"You are right. I will keep digging, maybe I can find some contact information and see how long this guy was employed and do a little work-up on him," Jones was already searching contact numbers for the APEX human resources office.

Terri returned to the task of evaluating the photographs while Jones busied himself with his self-assigned responsibility.

"Where do you guys come up with that nonsense? Do you believe the company he worked for would provide a clue to the killer? How many employees do you think there are at APEX?" Cooper was skeptical, almost shrugging off the lead.

"There is nothing in these pictures worth noting. Nothing is standing out to me," Cooper remarked.

"Yeah, I know, I keep hoping there is something though," Terri centered in on a photo of the body.

"He captured a lot of detail. Yes, he did nice work. Although, I would have probably used a different angle." Cooper retorted.

"Do you see this? Is that a smudge on his face? Right here, next to his jaw?" Terri thought it might have been dirt, but it seemed to be a funny shade, "Maybe it is a birthmark?"

"Terri picked up the third sealed envelope on the desk, "AUTOPSY PHOTOGRAPHS- DO NOT BEND 029-612-06," she read. She cleared a section of her desk to pull them out and lay them on a flat surface, still forgetting about the express envelope from New York.

He looked kind of young with a soft, bloated unshaven face. *His hair was short and brown. Who did you piss off? What happened to you?* Terri asked herself.

His ears were pierced with one earring missing.

There were several x-ray photos of his skull and throat. It appeared a blunt heavy object crushed in his trachea. Distinctive black and blue strike marks turned a deep, dark red across his neck. *He was unconscious in seconds, dead in minutes.*

"This is it, this little blue smudge. Doesn't it look like eye shadow or something?" Terri searched the top drawer for a magnifying glass."

"Let me see," Jones held the photo close to his face, "yeah, looks like eye shadow. Maybe this guy was a cross dresser."

"I think it looks more like chalk, do you see that?" Terri stated.

"Randy, could you get me a copy of his property items, the ones we found on him? And while you are up, have Jack run his criminal history and print the sex offender information on his last known address," she knew he would do it immediately.

Jones exited and returned to Terri's office with printed sheets of paper within minutes, "Terri – get this. 51172 Monica Street. He had registered at Moore's address. He changed his address three months ago, verified here and last week for the new verification period, he changed it to 123 Homeless. His criminal history is rich with convictions involving sex with persons under the age of 13. He had been released on parole, and the Monica address was his only registered address out of prison. He was reported as a parole absconder seven days ago by his Parole Officer."

"Get on the phone to the PO and find out if he went to the address. Maybe he knows something," Terri told him.

"Just what would a PO know about the dead guy other than he was supposed to report?" Cooper took his turn asking questions.

"David, he might know who his friends are and what his other hobbies are. We have to learn more about him so we can build a better picture," Terri thought he should know that already.

"Here is that list of property items you asked for, nothing really special," Jones stated.

"One diamond-like earring, a business card, cash, wallet, car keys, I don't see anything unusual about his possessions," Cooper had taken the list.

"Maybe they played pool, Terri. Just a thought, maybe there is a pool league around here that we don't know about," Cooper retorted.

"Maybe we should find out what vehicle he owned and where he parked it?" Terri suggested.

Jones asked her, "Don't we have keys from Kramer, too. Did we ever find his vehicle?"

"No, not yet. Get a work-up on what they were driving and let's see if we can't find those vehicles. Obviously, there were no cars parked in the driveway on Monica." She instructed Jones to complete a vehicle history on both of them.

"This other guy, Hines. I'm going to start doing some checking on him also. I jotted his name down, but I haven't done a work up yet. But first, I think I'll get out of here for a minute and drive down the parole office and see if we can get physical copies of any information they have on Kramer. I'll call Jess, too," he started for the door.

"Randy, just because he was a sex offender doesn't mean he deserved to die. Someone murdered him," Terri looked down through the criminal history, "and I would say they may have had a good reason."

"I'm not saying he deserved to be killed, but if it were my daughter..." Jones could not hide the sheer disgust; there was no need for him to finish his statement.

He left the office stopping Pierce in the hallway. "Come on bud; I'll fill you in on the way to the parole office."

Cooper passed both of them on his way to the kitchen, but neither offered an invite.

"I'm going to head out, too, Terri. I have a couple of errands to run," Cooper told her.

Terri stayed behind, trying to make sense of it all.

Chapter 10

"Honey, I'm glad you are finally home. You haven't eaten all day, you're tired, and it's quarter to twelve," Ryann could see Terri was still a little wired up from her busy day.

"Sit down, honey, eat your dinner, relax," she tried getting her to sit at the dining room table. She placed her drink in front of her plate.

"I think I'll eat in the living room," Terri grabbed her drink and headed for the living room.

Ryann followed her with the plate and watched as she sat on the sofa, picked up the remote and began flipping aimlessly through channels. Duke started barking at the back door, so Ryann took the opportunity to give Terri a little breathing room and let him outside.

When she walked back into the room, she asked, "Do you want me to stay tonight?" She was already kneeling down to take off Terri's boots and socks. She started to rub her bare feet before Terri answered.

"Yeah, if you want," not realizing she was hurting her feelings. Ryann couldn't believe she was having such a hard time getting this woman to open up to her. She was a tough nut. Strong, confident, she definitely did not let anyone in her life she wasn't ready to let in.

"Will you let Duke back in please, I don't know what the hell he's barking at, and the neighbors are going to get pissed, it's late," Terri asked, too tired to get up.

"I will try, but he has been chasing those rabbits lately and won't come in for me," Ryann stood up to try again.

Duke bounced from the shrubs near the neighbor's property, still barking, he didn't want to leave his fixed position, "Duke! Get your ass in here, now!" She yelled a little louder this time.

He finally ran up to the door, the hair on his back

standing up near his tail, "Leave them damn rabbits alone, fool!" She muttered as she patted his back to calm him down.

She leaned over to kiss his nose but remembered his training. She knew he was used to her scent by now, but she still did not trust him. Ryann looked out into the yard and saw nothing but the moonlight casting shadows across the lawn.

She turned back, her eyes focused on Terri. She was so beautiful. She caught herself standing at the sliding glass door, staring.

"What?" Terri was staring back.

"Just looking," Ryann replied as she made her way to the couch. She curled up next to her and grabbed a blanket.

"You want to talk about something this evening?" Ryann asked as politely and softly as possible, trying not to sound like she is prying or hurt.

"What do you want to talk about?" Terri raised her voice to speak over the television, "You know what? Let me change, get out of these clothes."

Terri changed into comfortable running pants and a t-shirt, "What do you want to talk about?" she asked again, walking through to the living room and sitting at the edge of the couch before sliding off the arm and melting into a cushion. She was not prepared to divulge personal details about her life, and she hoped Ryann wasn't going to ask.

Ryann sat down next to her and asked, as if for the first time, "How was your day?"

Terri answered, "Long and exhausting, mentally."

"How was yours?" she deferred.

"Well, what did you do today? Who did you talk to? How was your partner?" Ryann began a wealth of standard questions, but Terri felt she was being interrogated.

"What, you don't think I was at work?"

Ryann backtracked and tried to explain, "No, I think you did go to work. We have been seeing each other for almost three months and I hardly know anything about what you do, how your work day goes, or even if your partner is married, and yet he probably knows everything about me."

"I don't talk about you at work, and I definitely don't talk to David about you or anyone. I don't like to talk about work; I don't know what to say. Most of the stuff I do I can't tell you, and the rest is just boring," Terri drank half the beer in two long gulps.

"Why don't you just talk to me about your partner then, David?" Ryann stood to get Terri a second beer and one for herself. Returning from the kitchen with two cold ones, Ryann offered a solution, "Maybe if we talk about David then you won't feel like you are sharing information with me about work, you would just be telling me about your partner."

Terri took the beer and a few sips. She sat back and pulled her legs up on the couch getting more comfortable. She was contemplating the conversation, she really didn't know very much about Ryann either, and she reviewed what she did know quickly. *We met at Bob's Bar during a friends work party. We had periodic conversations about running and rock climbing. You love dogs, so Duke was not a bother. The highlight of our activities had been ice-cold beverages, long evenings, and sex.* Terri reflected on their previous conversations.

"Oh, I don't know, maybe you could ask me some questions?" Terri started.

"Ok, you know the questions I want to ask are about work, though? You know I am super curious about your job – it is something I could never do," Ryann inquired.

"Ok, what would you like to know?" Terri said, a little more relaxed having consumed the second beer.

"You want another one, babe?" Ryann got up to get another one for herself. She was a little nervous, but she would be strategic about what she would get Terri to tell her.

"Yeah, why not," Terri looked at her empty bottle

and waited for Ryann to bring her the new cold one. She was nearly inhaling them this evening.

"Ok," Ryann sat across from her on the couch, each of them leaning against the arm, facing one another. She pulled the blanket over both of them for warmth.

"Have you ever shot anyone?" Ryann asked her first work-related question.

"Uh, thank God – No," Terri said, "there have been a couple of times where I have been very close to pulling the trigger, and for whatever reason, I didn't do it, I just could not pull the trigger."

"Why not? What happened?" Ryann probed.

"I don't like to talk about it. I should have shot the bastard, I thought he had a gun, and we were wrestling, but I did not shoot. I am sure I could have been exonerated, but I will never know," Terri twitched a bit, took a deep breath and exhaled.

"It was a simple and routine traffic stop. A young man, I believe he was 17 at the time, I stopped him for speeding near the school," Terri recalled the traffic stop vividly.

"He was driving a black four-door Ford Crown Victoria. The windows were tinted and he stopped in the middle of the road," she took another sip. She looked nervous just retelling the story, but she found herself wanting to talk about it. "Anyway, I called out the stop and asked for backup. It felt like something wasn't right, just by the way he stopped his car, right in the middle of the road."

"Oh, wow. See that is something I would never think to pay attention to," Ryann appeared marveled at Terri's deduction of danger.

"I walked up to the car. The young man opened his driver door and plowed right into me!" Terri was digging her toes into the couch cushion.

"What about Duke?" Ryann asked.

"He stays in the car unless I need him. I just don't have time to have him walk up to the car with me like a regular partner. Anyway, he must have seen it because he went totally crazy. He was howling and barking; I remember hearing him in the distance." Terri placed herself back at the moment.

"I was able to stay on my feet, but he grabbed for something in his pocket. I don't think I had ever been more frightened," she sipped her beer slowly this time.

"Oh my God! What was in his pocket, how did you get him, were you hurt?" Ryann was at the edge of her seat, peeling the label from her bottle beer.

"I'm not sure after that; it was such a blur. He tried to grab my gun, but I got to it first. When I pulled it out of the holster I yelled at him to lay on the ground, I thought the volume of my voice would have shaken the neighborhood, I was yelling so loud," she took a long swallow, her throat growing dry.

"It was then I realized he already had something in his hand. I saw a flash of light, but it was the overhead emergency lights from my patrol vehicle reflecting from his cellphone," Terri stared at the television as though she were watching it unfold again.

"For a moment, I thought he was trying to disarm me, and then I believed he had pulled a small .22 caliber pistol from his pocket. I heard the distant wail of sirens; my backup was on the way. I must have hit the emergency button on my portable radio during the struggle."

"Where were you? I mean, was anyone around to help you?" Ryann asked.

"We were right downtown, and there were several witnesses, but no one helped. I was told later that one of the onlookers did call 911 and tell them an officer was in a fight. I still don't know who made that call. Anyway, David showed up, and the young man gave up. David doesn't let me live that down. He always reminds me how he 'saved my life.' You know that asshole had coffee spilled down the front of his uniform shirt when he showed up?" Terri's face grew into a shade of pinkish red.

"Where was he? Wasn't he supposed to be with

you?" Ryann wondered if the traffic stop would have had the same outcome had her partner been with her.

"I don't know where he was. But after that, Captain Williams assigned David to work in the car with me directly. I guess you could say she assigned partners after that incident," Terri explained.

"I bet you were scared. I mean I would have been shitting my pants!" Ryann empathized with the situation, the hair on her arms raised in a fuzz of gooseflesh.

"Honestly, it seemed like a slap in the face when David became my partner. I didn't need him, I handled my own, and I already had Duke."

"Okay, okay. What's the next question?" Terri moved and stretched out along the edge of the couch to make herself more comfortable. She practically placed her feet on Ryann's lap for her to rub.

Good. That's a start, Ryann thought before asking the next question. "Ok, well what about the most interesting case you have ever handled?" She asked, not willing to give up on the conversation with Terri.

"Terri?" Ryann repeated, waiting for acknowledgment.

"Terri? Snap out of it. If you don't want to talk about it anymore, just say so," she was disappointed.

Terri found herself trapped in a reflective glance, ignoring the question, and unable to continue.

"Terri, this is the problem. We have a chance you could tell me anything, about anything, and all I want is for you to talk to me, about anything," Ryann was frustrated.

"I will; I just can't remember anything specific. I live it every day," Terri was trying to explain that she really didn't want to talk. That she would rather not face anxieties or fears about her job. That would mean failure, letting her job get the best of her. Ryann took one last opportunity to dig for information, and she used a subject matter Terri just might be able to talk about.

"What about any gory crashes?"

Terri sighed, "Well, we have really only had a couple of crashes, but I will tell you the most accident-prone location is that right turn on Stern Creek Road. There was a horrible crash there last year where two people were killed. It was my partner's wife and daughter," Terri was staring off again as if replaying the scene in her visual memory bank before she spoke again.

"David?" Ryann asked.

Terri continued to talk, ignoring the question, "As I remember that incident, David was the first one on the scene. What a horrific sight it must have been for him. He still doesn't talk about it."

She began to recall the events as she remembered starting with the dispatched call, "I was across town headed in when the dispatcher put out that a passerby reported headlights in the trees off Stern Creek Road, near McGuire. David was the closest, and he said he would roll by and take a look since he was on his way home. He drove to the part on Stern Creek Road where it makes that sharp right angle turn, and he must have seen the headlights off in the ditch. It was last year about this same time when the fluctuations in the weather cause the temperature to change enough to bring about a soup of fog," Terri told her. She was staring at a small crack in the wall near the window.

"Earlier in the week, another vehicle had wiped out the right angle warning sign and 15 mph caution blinker. Waterford being as small as it is, doesn't generate the kind of revenue necessary to keep the roads maintained and replace all the felled signs, so the car in the ditch must not have been ready for the turn either."

Terri was gripping her beer bottle tightly when Ryann reached over and loosened the tension of her fingers, "Go, on," she said.

"It was close to midnight, and it was dark in that area, so I headed his way just in case he needed help with lights for the road," Terri tried to describe her anxiety as she drove to the venue, but Ryann could see the color draining from her face.

119

"I recall the dispatcher asked him if he needed a wrecker and the next thing you heard was David sounding completely unnerved. His voice was trembling, and something was very wrong – and everybody knew it. He called for the ambulance and a fire truck and backup. He screamed into the microphone that she was trapped and non-responsive and he smelled gasoline. He was talking so fast; he sounded frantic."

Terri was reliving the past, "I piped up that I was almost to the bend on Stern Creek and I could see his vehicle and a huge plume of smoke. I remembered cursing that downed sign and the repeated complaints from locals. I pulled up lights and sirens blazing, skidded to a stop next to David's patrol car," she was still staring off into the memory.

"I had never seen such a fire! I pounced out of my patrol car and began to run toward the inferno, but David stopped me. He was mumbling that the fire was too hot and it was too late. I stood in disbelief- the vehicle was totally engulfed. David was crying and furious at the same time," Terri remembered.

"I asked him why he was so upset. At first, I thought it was that he felt so helpless while we watched the orange balls of fire," but he could not talk, he only stared.

"Who was it? I had asked him. David was incredibly upset. He never acted like that on any other crashes or dead dogs or shooting injured deer for that matter. I thought maybe it was because he was actually talking to the driver and maybe he tried to get her out, and that bothered him."

Terri grew stiff while she spoke, "But then, David kept marching around, stomping his feet, until he slumped to his knees in front of my car. It turned out the car was David's, and his wife Rebecca was driving. Their five-year-old daughter Hayley was in the car, too," Terri explained.

"David was distraught and couldn't talk, and he insisted on completing the report himself. He said it would help him heal. He stood around the scene until well after the fire trucks and the coroner had gone. He insisted on taking the scene photographs and reconstructing the crash events. He was the Accident Reconstructionist and still is the only one we have." Terri was certified in accident investigations, but had not had the training required to 'reconstruct' crash scenes.

"What? Oh, my God. Are you kidding me?" Ryann was pressing Terri to see if she could keep her talking, "What about the 911 caller didn't the 911 caller stop to help?"

"I don't really know. The 911 caller never gave their name or number, and we did not know who actually made the call. Maybe they were worried that since they didn't help after witnessing it, they could be held responsible," she told her.

"I could not imagine. There is no way I would be able to function. Did he talk to her before she died?" Ryann pressed Terri on the memory.

"The station was in a whirlwind for several days. David would not take time off except for the actual day of the funeral. It always bothered us how he refused any help, but we understood how personal this was for him and he needed to do things his way, so he could have closure." Terri recalled how David refused help investigating the crash, and to her, it seemed relatively straightforward.

"The final report revealed she was driving way too fast, lost control on the curve in the gravel, left the roadway and rolled her car several times. He had said the vehicle struck a buried utility marker and it appeared the sparks started a fire and quickly engulfed the car in flames. Rebecca's body was so badly burned, it was beyond recognition, only DNA found in her teeth and bones were available for identification. The same was true for Hayley, she was in a child seat in the back," Terri's eyes were glued to a spot on the floor again.

"Geesh. Her mother must have been devastated, losing a daughter and grandchild," Ryann empathized with Rebecca's family.

"I don't know. I didn't see anyone from her family at the funeral. David said she didn't have any family. He hasn't talked much about it since, and he didn't dare talk about Rebecca to anyone. In fact, it was rumored that he had taken a substantial life insurance policy out on her, but no one ever knew if or what they paid – or even if it was true."

Terri continued, "He didn't start taking time off work until last year. He started taking Fridays and Mondays off. He bought a new car and went on trips out of town. But he is a private man, even for us being partners, he doesn't confide in me about much." Terri found herself explaining his introverted behaviors.

"Life insurance policy?" Ryann was prying.

"I heard there was, but I don't think there was one, or David probably wouldn't be working. He is incredibly lazy, and I can safely assume he would be too lazy to even get quotes on a policy," Terri explained.

"So, what part of the investigation did you take part in?" She again pressed Terri.

"Come to think of it, not much. I held the end of a tape measure after standing where David told me to stand. I took photographs and helped the fire department clean up the road when we were done taking the reconstruction measurements. That's about it, it was nothing really." Terri confessed she had let David do most of the work in the investigation. She sat quietly, remembering how he had insisted he do it because Rebecca was his wife and he owed it to her and Hayley.

"What was the cause of death?" Ryann was curious.

"Why are you asking me these questions?" Terri asked.

"I mean, was it the crash or the fire?" Ryann asked.

"I don't really know, and nobody really talked about it. I assumed they died on impact because David said they were non-responsive," Terri relayed the events just as if David were telling Ryann himself.

"I guess he did try to talk to them. What about the autopsy?" Ryann inquired.

"There was no autopsy, the bodies were so badly burned they were cremated, besides I think we all just assumed. The funeral was at Coats Funeral home in town, and the whole police department was there. Why?" It was Terri's turn to ask questions.

"Why was she driving out there anyway, so fast I mean, was she doing something or going somewhere? I think it is super interesting. Don't you?" Ryann tried to aim the inquisition back toward Terri.

"I don't think there was ever a question," Terri responded, finishing off the last of her beer, "Why?"

"I remember reading something about it in the paper, the paper said she was driving at least 50 mph, but if she had driven that way before, she would have known that corner was there and slowed down. The paper said the whole car burned up, but did anyone ever look at it?" Ryann pushed for information.

Terri was fidgety and moved her feet back to the floor. Ryann patted her lap and reached for Terri's feet, but they were a bit too far.

"That's weird, I never thought about it. David did the vehicle inspection; he is much better at it than I am." It seemed Terri's wheels were spinning and she ignored the invite, "You can't believe everything you read in the paper, and definitely not from a small town gossip line. Why are you asking me anyway?"

Terri swung her feet back up to Ryann's lap, then back to the floor.

Ryann sensed Terri was still anxious about the incident, "I don't know. I'm excited you are talking to me, sharing with me something and I am curious in a non-cop kind of way, you know?" Ryann said, "Now give me back your feet."

She gave her a soft reassuring tone, "I told you I want to know more about you. What makes you tick? A little insight as to who you are, I just wanted you to talk to me, and I don't care what it is about."

"I guess I've never dated anyone who had more questions than you have. Maybe no one ever wanted to talk about my work before, at least not the way you are asking, I mean, it seems like, well, like you care about my feelings," Terri's eyes were watering.

"Okay, next question then. That's enough about work, besides we have better things to talk about," Ryann said with a smirk. "Let me get some lotion for your feet; they are calloused pretty badly. It must be those boots you wear."

"No, no it's ok. I would rather not; it is already very late. Why don't you come here, babe, let me hold you," Terri reached up and pulled Ryann toward her, and before too long they were both asleep.

Chapter 11

Terri was up early and decided she would head to work. She parked in the side lot next to the building, and she was the first person to arrive. She disarmed the building alarm and headed for the back offices.

She stopped at the mini kitchen and started the coffee. *It has to be a little stronger this morning,* Terri thought. She reflected on her late evening talk with Ryann. They had fallen asleep in an awkward position, and she had never gotten comfortable. Terri felt as though she hadn't slept at all.

Terri made her way to her cubicle and sat down at the desk as cymbals chimed from her hip pocket. "This is Terri," she said coldly into the phone, not realizing how she sounded.

"Hey, boss. I just wanted to know if you are headed to the office today. You know we have the complete coroner report including blood analysis, and I printed all of the law enforcement criminal history on Kevin Kramer. I thought we could pull out the photographs today and just look at them for a minute. There has to be something we are overlooking," Jones was eager to solve the homicides.

"I'm already here Randy, come in. We will talk about it. I want to get the work up you already did on Hines, too." The Kevin Kramer homicide was weighing heavily on her mind, but now that Jones wanted to go over it, she would have a chance to review the scene once again.

"Do I need to bring you a donut?" Jones joked, "You sound terrible," he was hoping the gesture would lighten her temperament.

"The coffee is on, and I'm trying to be patient. If I were you I would wait about 20 minutes," Terri hoped her depressive mood would wear off by the time he got to the office. She was having a difficult time shaking the fatigue, but she knew better than to take it out on Jones.

"Maybe you could bring me a choco-dip?" He could hear the smirk in her voice.

"Sure thing! I'll bring a dozen," he was happy to oblige.

Terri grabbed her cup and made her way to the break room. The coffee had finished the last brew cycle and she barely poured the first cup when her office phone rang. *The voicemail will get it,* she hoped. After the fourth ring, it stopped. She added a little cold water in her cup, so the coffee was a tolerable temperature. She returned to her desk and sat facing the "Kevin Kramer" folder of information.

Where to begin? She thought. Her desk phone rang. Looking at the incoming caller identification display, she saw it was a direct dial from the outside.

The office wasn't open for another 30 minutes, and she fought the urge to answer it. After four rings, the caller was sent to voicemail. She waited a few minutes then picked up the phone to listen to the message, but cymbals sounded from her cell phone and she hung up.

She checked the Caller ID: David Cooper, "Good morning, David," Terri acknowledged her partners' call instead.

"I know you are in the office, I drove by and saw your car. Why didn't you answer the phone?" He sounded tired.

"We aren't open yet, are we?" She was just as miserable as he was.

Cooper cut straight to the point, "I'm not coming into the office this morning. I have some errands to run, and I want to talk to that teenager across from Mrs. Peck. I think he may be the guy we are looking for on those mailbox complaints." He offered an excuse, but no one ever really checked up on him. "When I get back, maybe we could look over what you have on the Kramer and Moore incidents. I would like to read over the notes for myself."

"Randy is coming in and we are going to look over the autopsy reports this morning. We are going to try and sift through some photographs also. We will probably head out to the scene and see what we can gather. We may have missed something."

"Terri, why don't you wait until I get in and then you can fill me in, and I can look over it all with you guys?" Cooper was more telling than asking.

"No, Randy will be here soon, and we are going over the information. I think he has a profile on him from the FBI that I would like to see," Terri told him. She was getting irritated at the way Cooper always insisted on being the lead investigator on every major case.

"Whatever Terri. You know you are going to end up asking me about it anyway. You always do." He reminded her how they collaborated on most investigations.

"Getting your feedback and working as a team is much different than you running the whole show, David." Her depressed mood turned to pissiness, "I will let you know if we need anything," she hung up and sipped on her coffee. Her aggravation made her get up and walk around to the window. *Driving by to see if I am here and didn't stop in. He is weird.*

She released a little tension with a few leg squats when she saw Randy pull in the parking lot. *Thank God, a person with some ambition and humility.* She hadn't realized how thankful she was for the last couple of weeks when Cooper was on vacation.

Jones entered the back door, and Jack was at his heels.

"Hey Jack, you are in early this morning," Terri remarked, "I didn't see you pull in."

"Um, morning Terri," Jack said, "It's only 30 minutes early, besides I was up early anyway. That damn rooster crows at the earliest hours." Jack was proud of his "small farm" consisting of a few chickens and an obnoxious cock.

"Coffee is already made if you guys want some, and Randy brought the donuts," Terri spied the donut shop bag.

"Good thing or I would have to send him back out," Jack teased him.

Jones turned and replied, "I hope you brought lunch today, I am planning on being busy. With Officer Reese working today I thought you could dispatch him to all the complaints so Terri and I could work on the Kramer case," Jones was hopeful.

"I thought Officer Cooper was back? Isn't he going to want to work with Terri? Everyone knows Cooper is a fucking prick when his routine is interrupted," as usual, Jack's filter did not allow him to speak politely.

"He called me already. He said he was going to be following up on a lead on the mailbox destruction case this morning and probably wouldn't be in until late afternoon," Terri relayed her earlier conversation with him.

"That's fucked up. We get a couple of homicides, and the man who can find a needle in a haystack isn't on the case. What the fuck is wrong with him? Afraid of working a damn real case?" Jack was ruthless. His words turned to mumbles as he stuffed a raspberry filled donut in his mouth.

"Jones and I are going to be in the conference room for a couple of hours. If something comes up and Reese can't handle it alone, let us know, please. I think he is on until 2," she had already started down the hall.

"Sure thing, but not for another 26 minutes!" Jack walked into the break room and helped himself to another donut and topped off his coffee.

"Thanks for the donuts, Jones," he stuffed half of the second one in his mouth and headed to the front dispatch center.

Jones grabbed his coffee and threw in three large spoons of sugar, "Terri! Wait up! I'll be right behind you. Do you have all the files? I'll meet you in the conference room. I have to take a leak." Jones was trying to contain his excitement, but he still had to use the bathroom. He hurried then ran back to the cubes where he found Terri still at her desk.

"Jess said she had some work done the Hines guy, and I have to download the PDF file she emailed me," he told her.

"Good. I will bring the photographs and scene sketches down to the conference room. Oh, is Mike coming in today?" She asked.

"I think he said something about coming in. Let me check his desk calendar; he is pretty anal about 'listing' his work times," he was already hovering over Pierce's desk in search of the information.

"Off," Jones said then grabbed a folder highlighted with the case number and the name Kevin William Kramer.

Terri gathered her files and waited for Jones to download and print the PDF from Jessica.

"Let's shove these two tables together and see if we can't get these photos laid out like the scene," Terri suggested once the finally made it to the conference room.

"I'll be right back," Jones set his items down and returned a few minutes later with his office whiteboard and some markers.

"You know I am a visual person; I think this will help me understand where we are," Terri had already divided the paperwork into three piles: Autopsy, Crime Scene Photos, and Personal Information.

"I told you not a good idea to start without me boys," Cooper made his entrance into the conference room. "I told you I did not want to miss any of the meetings on the homicides," he hovered the table arrogantly then pulled up a chair.

"I'm not a 'boy' asshole," Terri corrected him. "Now that you have decided to join us, I guess I'll read some of the information that we had already gone over so you can catch up," Terri was not impressed.

"Randy, let's start with autopsy results," he took

his black marker and scribbled "Manner of Death" at the left corner and drew a line beneath it, "Ok, let's hear it."

"The coroner has determined the manner of death to be Criminal Homicide due to asphyxiation. The anterior portion of the neck containing the pharynx and larynx are markedly crushed on the right side of the neck due to blunt force trauma."

Terri continued reading from the report, "It is possible that strangulation could cause such an injury, however internal injuries consisted of subcutaneous connective tissues of the throat and neck extravasated blood with blood noted in the mouth. There are obvious notable fragments of the hyoid bone embedded along the esophageal wall. The muscles of the neck revealed blood on the anterolateral position. The larynx showed a fracture of the cricoid cartilage, right side, and anterior aspect close to the anterior midline. The absence of subconjuctival hemorrhaging of the eyes, ligature marks, scrapes or abrasions on the exterior of the skin indicative of strangulation all but eliminate the possibility of strangling."

Terri scanned the rest of the medical jargon and repeated, "Blunt Force Trauma causing Death."

"Seriously, Terri? Like Moore? I mean Moore and Kramer were killed the same way? So they were struck on the left side of his neck?" Jones questioned, "So the killer was probably left-handed?"

"Holy fuck. Do you think it could have been that half of pool stick we collected from the Moore scene?" Jones was asking what Terri was already thinking. He pulled some photos out to spread them on the table. "We never did find the other half, did we?"

Cooper clarified, "Blunt object to the throat with enough force to kill a man. Whoever it was sounds like they were pretty damn angry."

"Hold on, let me get through some of these other descriptions." Terri continued, "The nails of the hands were manicured and clean and were swabbed for the possible presence of DNA materials with none being found."

"Okay, so he didn't fight back or get his hands on the suspect...at least not that we know of," she stated.

Jones wrote on the board – 'blunt force trauma: left-handed suspect' beneath the first heading.

"The rest of the autopsy explains his cardiovascular system, respiratory system, hematopoietic, Gastrointestinal, Biliary, Genitourinary, Endocrine, Musculoskeletal, and Central Nervous Systems. It seemed there was nothing abnormal about any of that," Terri summed up the remainder of the autopsy report.

"Is the toxicology report included in the autopsy or did we have a separate laboratory analysis for that?" Cooper asked.

"I believe there is a toxicology report as well, just a second," Terri sifted through the pages to find the heading 'Toxicology.'

"Yes, here it is. Blood Ethanol: Negative. Drug Screen: Ibuprofen and Caffeine detected."

"No alcohol or drugs?" Cooper sounded surprised.

"The opinion of the medical examiner is that Kevin W. Kramer, Caucasian male, 05/11/1984, died due to asphyxia, secondary to laryngeal trauma, secondary to blunt force trauma to the neck. He had not been consuming alcoholic beverages prior to his death, nor had he ingested controlled substances. The manner of death is classified as a homicide," Terri read the final opinion.

"Did you complete the work-up file on this guy?" Terri wanted to see the information Jones had finished when they first received the identification report from the latent print unit.

"Kevin William Kramer, 37-year-old white male, 5' 6" / 165 lbs., brown hair, and green eyes. No known tattoos, ear piercings in both ears. His driver's license expired in 2010, and it was also suspended and revoked. He had a state-issued identification card with his last address of 51172 Monica, Waterford," Jones began.

"He had a significant criminal history, Terri. It looks like it dates back from 2009 when he spent time in a juvenile jail in Virginia for fraudulent activities. The next is all drug related and sex crimes in 2010 in Georgia, and again in Pennsylvania in 2011."

"Maybe our boy likes to party and got himself into a little of trouble along the way?" Terri assumed. She focused on the autopsy report.

"In 2009 he was arrested again on drug trafficking and possession of child pornography in New York. One more time in 2011 for criminal sexual conduct involving a minor. His record is clean after that, so I am guessing he spent some time in prison on the last charge, at least until recently."

Jones continued, "He was listed as an absconder from parole out of North Carolina and has several outstanding warrants for his arrest on other pornography-related charges."

"Nice, guy," Terri smirked, "was he supposed to be registering in this county?"

"Apparently he was, Terri. His last known address was on Monica Street where we found Moore. He was definitely using that address, but I don't think he lived there at all," Jones told her.

"Wait a moment, Jones," Cooper piped up. "Terri, isn't that the registered address of the other guy you found dead? They were both registering at the address also?" Cooper tried to appear genuinely interested, but he was staring out the window, apparently fixated on a squirrel running the Maple tree.

"Yes, that's the address where Moore was murdered. Randy, Mike, and I were there."

"We already have the names of the people that were supposed to be living there, and I also contacted the homeowners, the Donnelly's. I talked to Barb Donnelly on the phone, and she was in Florida with her husband. They were gone most of the time. She told me she and her husband were the only ones who live there and they didn't have renters or children that would visit," Terri provided a brief synopsis of her conversation with the homeowners.

"I don't remember seeing our guy, I mean, Kramer on the address or the vehicle list. Run another query on that, would you Randy?" Terri wondered how they could have missed that name.

"I'll get right to it, and I haven't checked for his vehicle yet, so I'll do that too," Jones headed back to his office, then stopped and turned in the hall, "Terri, you think I should give Jess a call on this?"

"What about your other guy, Jeremy Hines?" Cooper asked, "Do you have any information on him?"

"We aren't there yet, David. We are just getting that together. I'm not sure if there is anything we can do about the address situation right now anyway. Let's just see what we come up with for names and vehicles."

"Jones, you are going to call your FBI friend? Jessica. Isn't that the one? What does she have to do with this case?" Cooper turned and faced him.

"Terri? Do you want me to call her?" He asked again.

"No, work on getting me the vehicle details first. Thanks Randy." Terri looked through the paperwork Jones had left behind. She walked to his dry erase board and wrote, 'Criminal History' in the center of the page. She listed out his offenses and years they were committed. The next heading she scrawled on the far top right of the board, 'Photographs.'

Cooper sat watching her in silence. He seemed puzzled by the amount of work she was putting into solving the homicides.

"Done. I have it here Terri," Jones had already returned to the conference room with the printed information on Kramer.

"The secretary of state only has four people using that address. The homeowners, I assume, are Barbara and Mark Donnelly. But two more men had also used the address. George Moore, and Kevin Kramer. The only person with a vehicle registered to the address is Mark

Donnelly. It looks like he has a travel trailer, passenger vehicle, and a boat registered to him."

"How is it these guys are using their address?" Jones inquired.

"Jones, if you were a convicted sex offender would you want your neighbors to know who you were? Or would you chose a place that looks lived in but vacant and borrows their address instead?" Cooper smirked. The clear violation of law conflicted with Jones's moral sense of honesty.

"The state sex offender registry has this huge loophole of trust. The one where we expect the convicted felon to be honest about where they live, what they drive if they have phones or computers and if there are children around?" Cooper told him.

"What?" Jones was naively stunned.

"Yeah, the same registry that expects the police to conduct residence and address checks of every registered offender within their county. Sure, we have you and Pierce, but sometimes the complaint calls, vacations, and daily patrols interfere with our limited manpower to knock on every door to ensure proper verification." Cooper offered excuses for the missed address verifications.

"I guess you are right. That seems to be what Pierce and I have been doing, trying to keep these guys honest," Jones replied. He was still listening as he wrote, '51172 Monica Street' under the criminal history heading. He also added, 'Fraud, Drugs, Sex Offender.'

"It amazes me you guys would care so much about convicted criminal sex offenders anyway," Cooper commented.

Terri ignored him. She sat back and looked at the board, "Randy, do you think the murderer could be a victim of one of these guys?"

"You mean the person he raped finally getting the justice they feel they deserve?" Jones asked.

"Yes, it could be a victim. But I suppose we have to find out who those victims were and if they were capable of such a thing. It was one thing to be vengeful, and quite another to be so disassociated that the only relief from the pain would be murder."

"Do you want to grab lunch or break out the crime scene photos first?" Terri knew better as soon as she had asked.

"Photos, let's do this. I want to see them," Jones had a renewed sense of excitement. He saw that Terri might need a Coke to get through the next session, so he excused himself to the break room and reappeared with two cold ones and peanut butter M & M's.

"Thanks a lot, asshole," Cooper never let anyone buy him a Coke, but was sure to say something if he didn't get one.

"Calm down, Coop. I would have gotten you something, but you are sitting there lost in the photographs and paperwork. I don't believe you want to help, you are just curious."

"Before we look at the photos, Jones, let's look at the inventory of his items." Terri handed him a copy of a photocopied personal inventory list from Kramer's body.

"Is this from the autopsy?" Jones asked.

"No, this is from the scene, but you're right, there should be a list with the autopsy also."

"Let me see that," Cooper again grabbed the inventory list.

Terri reached for the autopsy packet and thumbed through it until she found the sheet marked 'Personal Items'.

"Here it is. I am going to make a copy for you guys so we can go through them together."

She went to the front office and found the copier out of order. She was irritated that Jack hadn't done it last week when she had asked him to, "Jack, get this copier fixed today please?"

"Use the one in the Captain's office, it is open," Jack didn't bother to look away from the lobby television. She found the officer door unlocked and entered. The Captain would not be in until after noon. She made two copies of the inventory sheet and headed back to the conference room. Jones was busy writing the list of items on his dry erase board when she returned.

"Here guys. Let's make a dual list. One side with Moore's items, the other with Kramer's. Let's compare them, maybe we can find something that will point us to the killer," Terri explained a plan of attack.

Jones began writing while Terri read, "Let me read the evidence we collected from the Kramer scene: One long purple strand of ribbon, bi-fold wallet, and brown stuffed animal."

"That's it?" Cooper laughed "I hope you guys took photographs."

"We found a receipt in the wallet for the local Meijer and Pierce is getting the surveillance video. There was also a business card. Where is the copy of that card, Randy?"

"Whoa! APEX industries, it has a PO box for New York on it. No other information Terri, not even a phone number or website," Jones was looking at the copy.

"Apex Insurance Corporation, again?" Cooper seemed a little more interested than he had before.

"No, it says industry," Jones reviewed the paper once again, "and not out of Meacon Bend."

"Get Jessica on that, Randy. See if she can get us the information for APEX with the PO box, maybe there are branches of that business. We should be able to make some phone calls and see what he was up to. Maybe his work is somehow related," Terri stated.

She continued, "The autopsy report for Kramer lists: one light green Abercrombie T-shirt, men's medium, one pair of Levis, blue size 36-34; Hanes underwear, black size medium; one pair of black crew length socks, a brown leather-like belt size 36; and a silver colored Citizens watch with clasp, and one clear colored earring. Also one brown shoe, size 8."

"Insurance company? Both of these guys worked for the same insurance company maybe?" Cooper repeated the question; his face had grown pale.

Of all things to key in on, David has to remember the insurance part of it, Terri stood thinking while Jones wrote.

Jones looked over the whiteboard, "Did I miss anything?"

"Hold on a second, that's not it," Terri turned the page and kept reading: "Several small slivers of wood with an enamel based coating were removed from the skin on the neck. The thumb and index fingers of his right hand had trace amounts of blue colored chalk."

Jones stopped writing and immediately began flipping through the autopsy report for Moore. "Terri, Moore was killed with that pool cue, remember? It was severely splintered and broken in half. Do you think they could have been killed at the same place? In that house on Monica?"

"They were both killed on Monica? That is quite a leap, even for you Jones. What if one was dumped on Monica, and the other in your box?" Cooper was never helpful when it wasn't his idea first. This time it seemed he was trying to confuse the issue instead of help.

"I think we should head out to the house and see if we can't find anything we may have missed. In fact, let's get the judge to sign a search warrant for the house, just in case we do find something," Terri suggested.

"I think so, too. Maybe there are cigarette butts or gum wrappers or something," Jones was hopeful.

"I'm sure we combed the ground fairly thoroughly when we were out on Stern Creek the first time, so I think we should start with the Monica house," Terri suggested.

Cooper was standing quietly looking at the notes Jones had made.

"David. David. David!" Terri snapped her fingers to bring him out of his whiteboard trance, "Do you see something we missed?" She asked.

"I think that covers it. Let me know if you need anything from me," Cooper distanced himself from their investigation and left the conference room.

"Seriously, Terri. What has gotten into him?

Doesn't he want to help? He just wants the information and then jets?" Jones asked of her partner.

"I'm not sure, Randy. He has always been a little on the weird side. But since Rebecca died, he doesn't even want to come to work, and he is always out of town. I'm just glad he still shows up so I don't have to worry about him," Terri commented.

She continued, "That's okay though. If he is not going to be able to offer anything to help us solve these murders, then it is better he doesn't help. And you know what? Why don't we take some more photos out on Monica, and then look at all of the scene photos when we get back? Then we can stop and grab lunch, too," Terri stated to Jones, she was trying to ease Jones' disappointment in Cooper.

"Sounds good to me, I could certainly eat something," he slid his dry erase board to the corner of the conference room. They were headed for the door when Cooper stopped them in the hall.

"Let me know when you type up that search warrant, maybe I will go with you to search the house. A new set of eyes wouldn't hurt," he offered, but Terri couldn't tell if he was sincere.

"Why? We started this investigation when you weren't here David, and you haven't cared much about it until just now," Jones stated in a condescending tone.

"I thought you guys might be farther along, but I see, after the little demonstration on the whiteboard, you are going to need my help after all," Cooper was a pompous ass.

"What was the name of that insurance company? Maybe I can do the work-up on them and see what they have to say about your two guys?" Cooper offered to do a little leg work and insurance background investigation.

"You know what, I won't turn down your help, but we are going to lunch first, and you are not invited," Jones told him.

"Maybe I will head out to Stern Creek with you two. You know, get my eyes on the original crime scene.

Point out the items you guys didn't get the first time."

"We probably won't end up at Stern Creek because we have plenty of scene photographs from there, anyway," Jones told him. "Aren't you working on that mailbox caper?" Jones' short fuse was growing even shorter.

"That's enough you two. David, we are going to grab lunch them come back and type up the search warrant. If you are here, you can go with us," Terri knew this would be enough to get him off their backs, at least for the afternoon.

She and Jones headed out the door. "I'll drive," Terri said as they pointed toward Stern Creek Road.

Chapter 12

"Thanks for meeting me so early. I am sorry for the short notice," Allison had called Terri at 8 am. She requested to meet for breakfast to go over a couple of items she discovered during her crash investigation.

Terri seized the opportunity to meet with Allison and offered a small excuse for being distracted, "I've just been little busy and frustrated. I m normally up early. I've been having a difficult time getting some decent sleep lately."

She was actually drained. She had been out late with Jones on the Stern Creek curve and come up empty-handed. The prosecutor's office had also called at 7:00 am, and she had spent a good half-hour reviewing details for an upcoming drunk driving case.

Ryann had gone out of town on a meeting with a client and Trisha offered to watch Duke so she could sleep in.

It was just before nine and they were sitting at Malone's for the breakfast special.

"I know. I have been reading the local papers, and the murders have been on the news, also. But there really hasn't been much information," Allison felt Terri must be sensitive about the investigations. She reached forward and caressed her hand as she scanned the menu for something to eat.

Distracted by her smallest touch, Terri set the menu down, "You know I would rather just have a beer or two. I don't feel much like eating after all."

"Dear, you must eat. It is way too early to drink. Unless you want a Bloody Mary, but you must also eat,"

Allison ordered one for each of them when the waitress walked their way.

"You know I find it all very interesting. I always wanted to be a cop," she blinked and smiled. "I find murder fascinating. Do you believe it is a serial killer?"

Terri was lost for a moment in what Allison had just said, "Umm, well the paper is right about one thing, we have two murders in Waterford," she found herself opening up a little, but hesitant to discuss the details that linked the two crimes together. *Why would she think it was a serial killer? I don't think the paper said anything about the manner of death,* Terri thought.

"How do you do your investigations?" Allison was curious, "Do a group of officers get together and tag-team like CSI? Like those crime scene shows?"

"Kind of, except we don't really do all of our own work. I mean, the officers take the calls and then they call out the detectives. Sometimes our detectives, like myself, also shag dispatched calls. The detectives call out crime scene technicians if they are needed for major case crimes, such as breaking and entering and murder. The technicians are the ones who actually take the fingerprints, photographs, and sketches," Terri explained as the waitress returned to their table.

"Hi Ladies, have you decided what you will be eating?" she asked.

"I will actually have another one of these, Bev," she pointed to the empty Bloody Mary glass.

"Terri, you cannot just drink alcohol for breakfast. I'll bring you a western omelet with fries, no hash browns," Bev said flatly and then she turned to Allison.

Terri did not argue; she was hungry; she just had not felt like eating.

"I'll have the same," Allison agreed with Bev.

"Go on," she said to Terri, more curious than before.

"Where was I? Oh yeah, once the evidence is gathered by the crime scene techs, they forward that to the lab for analysis," Terri continued.

Bev was back to the table with the drinks and set them down between them.

"What kind of evidence could you get from the guy you found in that field? I mean, it was just that dead guy, right?" Allison asked.

"No, well. We do have the dead guy, but also the things that were with him. And then there is the box," Terri explained.

"The box?" Allison questioned.

"Yes, well, the box was collected in pieces after we photographed it. That way it could be transported to the lab for possible fingerprint analysis. The latent print division can use some special processes for developing prints on paper products. Depending on how long the box had been laying there, and the weather, there could be prints on the cardboard," Terri explained.

"So the killer could have left his prints on the box? What if you get like 20 prints, I mean what about all of the other people that had touched the box beside the killer?" The question was legitimate.

"First, we have to see if they can actually obtain prints, then they would have to have something to compare them to. Like employees from the facility where the box came from," Terri was not hopeful about prints from the box leading to the killer.

"Where is the lab?" Allison wondered, "How long did that take? Was it like taking it to the lab and getting an instant answer? When will you know if they were able to get prints?" She was testing Terri's knowledge of lab processes.

"Well, it is supposed to work like that, but we don't have a lab here in Waterford. We send all of our lab stuff to the State Police lab in Ashton. They usually take about two weeks to process prints and sometimes longer for other things," she sipped her beer and pulled out a napkin to set it upon.

Terri had taught crime scene investigations at the local college last year. Having to explain it again was reminding her of how much television skewed the public

142

perception.

"In murder cases, they try to rush the latent print examinations. But it could actually take weeks to learn the identity of a person, and that depends on if they have ever been entered into the database," Terri explained.

"Did you guys get prints from the box?" Allison asked, "Do you have a suspect?"

"The lab couldn't pull any prints from the box that had enough value for comparison, so the prints didn't do us any good. We also have the label on the box, but it was kind of torn," Terri told her.

"That's too bad. What did the label say?" Allison was watching Terri carefully.

"Something, 'EX,' somewhere from New York. But, seriously, there were so many businesses from New York that ended and began with 'EX' that was a no-go," Terri explained her frustration in finding the name of the company.

"Do you know who the victim is? I mean, the paper said it was a stranger to Waterford, how did you guys know that?" Allison asked.

Terri thought for a moment wondering if she had read the news articles in the paper Allison was referring to. "We printed the victim because he didn't have identification. It didn't take long for the lab to figure out who he was, based on the information from the database. Our victim had been arrested on multiple offenses."

"What database?" Allison questioned.

"It is a law enforcement database of fingerprints. It's technically called AFIS – or the Automated Fingerprint Identification System. It was designed to keep track of everyone who had been arrested for serious crimes. Not everyone is in it, only if they had been fingerprinted. The database should spit out a matching prints. It is actually more complicated than that. I mean, an expert must compare the prints and make sure they belong to the same person. That is what takes so much time," Terri explained.

Bev arrived with the omelets, "Water?" She

acknowledged the near emptiness of their glasses.

"Oh, no. Not for me, thank you," Allison responded with a smile.

Terri fought the urge to order another Bloody Mary, "Water sounds fine. Wait, a Diet Coke please."

"So what happens when the prints match?" Allison hoped to learn more about fingerprint science, more specifically, if fingerprints were found at any of the crime scenes.

Terri continued, "If the lab had recovered prints from any of the items at the scene, they would notify the detectives. Then we could formulate a plan to interview the possible suspect. Hopefully, get a confession from the suspect. Then it is up to the prosecutor and the judge."

"What do you mean, possible suspect?" Allison questioned the validity of the science, "I thought if the print matched, then you would have your person."

"Not quite, " Terri smiled.

"So do you guys have possible suspects on your cases? What if the prints don't have a match to someone in the database?"

"Honestly, we are still compiling information, and we really don't have suspects. We actually have very little. As I said, the only prints we have are the victim's prints. No other prints were located or lifted by the lab. We actually do not have suspects at all. In the meantime, it is our job to talk to all of the neighbors for any possible leads," hungrier than she thought, Terri managed to eat most of her breakfast food during her five-minute explanation.

She cleaned her plate and had an internal debate about the third drink. "Like I said, the print will only match possible people that have already been entered into the database. There was a good chance the print may not be attached to a name," Terri clarified.

"What about your person's prints?" She repeated the question.

Terri explained, "Our guy was identified. He was

144

definitely in the database."

"And the other guy?"

"The other guy had his identification left on him. Both guys had their wallets, but only the one guy had I.D. Which I find interesting, why would one guy have I.D. and the other guy not?"

"Good point, does that mean someone took it? Like they saved it? Maybe like a souvenir?" Allison asked.

"I am not sure, that is something I will talk with my partners about. I'm leaning towards, no, but we will see. I don't think the killer would take one souvenir and not the other. If he were collecting driver's licenses or identification cards, why would he have left the other one behind? That doesn't make sense to me," Terri was thinking about it.

"What if the killer took different souvenirs from each victim?"

Still pondering the idea, "Now, that is a thought."

"Maybe the neighbors saw something or someone," Allison hoped Terri would tell her the extent of their investigation thus far.

"No one saw anything," Terri answered and waved Bev down, "Thanks, Bev, I'm done."

Allison had barely touched her breakfast, "This is so interesting, and I could talk about your investigations all day."

Bev refilled the water glasses and asked, "Is this on your tab?"

"Yeah, I'll get it tonight, okay?" Terri had to run to her bank for some cash before she would be able to settle the tab.

"Oh, no, I can get it. Bring me the bill. I'll take care of it officer, my treat," Allison winked. "So, what happens now?"

"You mean with the investigation?" Terri wasn't sure if the wink was an invitation to move beyond the conversation or if she really wanted to talk more about the murder.

"I'm sorry. You probably don't want to talk about it. I'm just curious how it happened, how were they killed? I read about it in the paper they were both strangled," she urged Terri to divulge critical information.

"Did the paper say that? I'm not sure what the press release said. I have not read the complete coroner report," she lied. "It doesn't matter yet, anyway. We have to figure out what type of people they were, what kind of lifestyles they led, and then maybe we can figure out why they were killed. Then we have to figure out who may have killed them," she felt as though she was over-explaining.

"I heard someone at the bar talking about a calling card of some type," Allison prodded. "This is such a small town, you would be surprised how much you could learn at the pub."

"Calling card?" Terri had not heard the rumor.

"Yeah, a card of some sort that was left at both scenes. What was it? What did it say?" She asked.

Terri reviewed the evidence in her mind. She recalled the business cards, but she had not thought of them as 'calling cards.'

The thought interrupted by the cymbals of her ringing cell phone, "Just a sec," she said to Allison, placing her finger over her lips and motioning for her to remain quiet.

"This is Terri," she said into the receiver.

"Yes, ha! Sure, Randy. I'll be there in a few minutes." Terri smiled and explained, "I'm sorry, I have to head back to the office and let Randy in. One of my partners locked himself out of the county garage, and he needs some gear. After that, I'm going to head for home. I still have some stuff to do before I get back to work tomorrow, and drinking really isn't helping!"

"Besides, I have to look into the souvenir idea and those calling cards; I wonder if Randy has pictures of those?" Terri smiled and got up to leave.

"Some other time to talk about the crash investigation?" Allison asked.

Terri was preoccupied and didn't hear the question.

"Maybe we could have lunch this weekend?" Allison asked again.

"How about if I call you? I work all weekend, and I am just not sure of my schedule. I know I have to run Duke to the training center and drop him off for two weeks. I'm just not sure what day that will be right now." *Also, I don't know Ryann's schedule, and I don't want to mess that up – yet*, Terri finished the mental explanation. She picked up her car keys and left through the back door.

She pulled her truck in next to Jones' at the station, "Need these?" She dangled the keys.

"Yeah, I forgot mine at home, and I didn't want to drive all the way back," Jones told her.

"What brings you in that can't wait until tomorrow?"

"I was reviewing these files, and I think I stumbled on something. I wanted to check it out. I was trying to imagine how these two guys could be related, other than using the same address I mean," Jones took credit for an idea Jessica had planted.

He followed Terri down the hall to the cubicles. He picked up the evidence envelopes and pulled out the pictures from the crime scene of Moore.

"See Terri? This business card found in Moore's wallet. It's from some insurance company, but on the back, it says '2 Squared'. What do you suppose that means?" He asked.

"I'm not sure. Maybe it is some kind of calling card left by the killer?" she repeated what Allison had suggested.

"Calling card?"

"Yeah, maybe the killer is trying to give us clues as to who he is. But what does '2 Squared' mean?" Terri picked up the evidence folder marked 'Kramer'. Here is the picture of his business card. It is a little scratched off, but it also says 'Square' on it. Right? Isn't that what it says? A little smudged, but I believe it says '2 Squared'," she had no idea what it could have meant.

"I think you are right. It does look like '2 Squared'. Okay, now what?" Jones stood staring at the photographs.

"Why don't you see if Jessica won't help us? Maybe she can pour it into a database of some sort? Maybe a gang database?" Terri suggested.

"Good idea. I'll shoot her a text right now. Maybe she will be able to meet me later tonight since we are both off," he hoped.

Chapter 13

Terri pulled into her driveway and found Ryann sitting on the front porch. She was reading a woman's sport, and fitness magazine and Duke was lying at her feet. He was excited to see her and ran out to the car.

"Hi, buddy!" Terri's face lit up, and she knelt to acknowledge her faithful companion. "Ok, enough, enough!" She told him, and he turned to the porch.

"Hi, hon. I thought you were off today? I tried to call, but you didn't answer," Ryann asked.

"I am, but I had court today," Terri stated, *at least for the first hour. Why should I tell her about Allison? Nothing happened anyway.*

"Well, I brought over bagels and juice, but you were already gone. Duke and I enjoyed them! What happened that has got you so bummed?" Ryann noticed she seemed a little down.

"My victim did not show up in court today. We waited all morning for her to stroll in. We tried to call her, and even sent Officer Reese over to her house, but she wasn't there. At least she didn't answer the door. I spent the rest of the morning talking with prosecutors and the family of the victim about the case," Terri was trying to conceal her deceit and recalled a previous discussion with the prosecutor from last week.

"This guy should have been in jail a long time ago, and now the victim doesn't show up to court, and he failed to register his latest address. It took forever to arrest him the first time. Now, the judge granted us a stay, but we will have to track him down again," she completed the lie.

"Is that typical? I mean, that the victims don't show up? What kind of case is it? Ryann asked.

"The victim, who is coincidentally his girlfriend, does not want to prosecute," she aired her frustrations from a previous domestic violence case as she sat on the porch in front of Ryann's chair.

"Why don't you tell me about it," Ryann placed her hands on Terri's shoulders and began to dig her thumbs into her shoulder blades. Terri noticed the strength in her hands and was grateful for the attempted stress reliever.

"It's work stuff, it really shouldn't bother me, but sometimes it does," Terri didn't really want to try and remember a lie. Thankfully she was silenced by Ryann's warm mouth on her neck.

"You can tell me," she coaxed. She was squeezing the muscle in her shoulders a little harder. Terri kept talking hoping Ryann wouldn't stop; her hands were so magical. Terri's skin was now bumpy from the deep massage and soft kiss. Ryann's hands worked down across her shoulder and dug into her biceps.

"Go on," she whispered again into her ear, biting on the lobe and tugging gently.

Terri continued to ramble, most likely from the guilt of actually spending the morning with Allison. "It is a domestic violence complaint, but it should have bigger charges, anyway we were supposed to have the preliminary exam today," she said, sounding disheartened.

"He has managed to postpone the exam for nearly a year. We have been keeping careful tabs on him since then. But today, the victim didn't show up. I should have gone to her house and drove her in myself," Terri now thought that would have been a good idea. She didn't think about it last week when the court appearance had been scheduled. She really didn't want to discuss it, but since Ryann was working out the muscle kinks, she kept talking.

"Phone calls started coming into the front desk about this guy several months ago when he first registered as a sex offender. Also the 'Report a Creep' line had gotten at least ten leads on where this guy was supposed to be hiding out. Unfortunately, we have not been able to catch him at the false address to bring another charge."

"He is a registered sex offender? He has a girlfriend? Didn't she know?" Ryann kept massaging Terri's shoulders.

Feeling the comfort from Ryann's warm hands, she breathed a sigh of relaxation and continued, "We will be able to obtain a felony warrant for his failure to change his address, but I don't think we will find him at the address he last registered. We have our work cut out for us proving that he doesn't live there."

"What about the victim? Why doesn't she want to prosecute?" Ryann kissed the outside of her shoulder. She managed to lift Terri's t-shirt up across her back and over her head, with the arms now the only real part of her body left in the shirt. She was scratching long strokes down her back.

Entranced, Terri kept the information flowing, "This guy is a real piece of work. When the victim called 911, she had been beaten and raped. But she felt she deserved the sex abuse out of duty to her 'man.' At least we got her to let us arrest him on the domestic violence."

"What? Rape?" Ryann slowed the scratch and lifted her hands up to grasp the meat in Terri's shoulders.

"Why did he have to register if he wasn't charged with the crime?"

"He has to register from a previous conviction. He brutally raped his last girlfriend, but then she ended up pregnant. It was only because of her parents that we were able to get a minor sex crime conviction."

"Wow, hold old was the victim before she had gotten pregnant?" Ryann asked.

"She was 16. The initial report from the victim was vicious. She claimed to have been taken advantage of, and her parents made the original complaint. She was so young, barely the age of consent at the time," Terri talked about his previous offense.

"I thought you only had to be 16 to 'legally' have sex?" Ryann asked.

"True. Consensual sex. See; apparently, her

parents were not pleased because he was 15 years older than she was. They pursued it, and because their daughter was still their responsibility until she turned 17, the victim went along. Now the victim is 17, and she is pregnant again."

"The same man?"

"Yes, the same perpetrator. Sex offenders brainwash the young. Offer them freedom and money and anything they desire. They promise the toys, candy, flowers, dresses, puppies, whatever it takes until they trust them. Then once the victim trusts him- or her – they take advantage of them, and it becomes 'consensual'- at least in the mind of the victim," Terri explained. Her head dropped down enjoying the rub down.

"That's horrible. What about the victim from today? What if she doesn't testify against him?" Ryann brought Terri back to her alleged morning court conference.

"Like we explained to the parents, the case will get dismissed. We still have one more chance to get him, though. It will be the last time, and if the victim doesn't show up, it is over," Terri stated.

"What if the suspect is threatening the victim? Like forcing her not to testify?"

Inquisitively Ryann prodded, trying to keep Terri distracted, "Couldn't the police do something if she is scared? Like what if she can't testify?"

"We wouldn't know unless the victim told us. Like I said, she is pregnant now, and I doubt she will be willing to put her boyfriend in prison. Especially when she doesn't want to raise their child by herself," Terri rationalized for the victim.

"What about the parents? Wouldn't they try and help raise the child?" Ryann thought about her own parents that they would have done anything for their daughters and grandchild.

"Ryann, you have to try to understand. The victim had probably been told by her boyfriend one of two things: either her parents don't want him around, so they don't want her happy. That would make her believe that they do not support her and she would distance herself from their help. Or second, he has told her that if she goes back home or testifies against him, he will beat and kill her. He would do his best to separate her from her family so she can't think for herself."

"Wow. That sounds complicated and crazy. So she would be virtually out of touch with her family?" Ryann asked. *Things were kind of making sense for her now, that fucking prick,* Ryann thought.

"Yes, he would make sure she had as little to do with them as possible. Even worse, he would make her chose between his 'undying, everlasting' love and her parents. She would be forced to chose him or her friends, or other family members, or anyone else for that matter. It is sickening." Terri explained some of the psychology behind victimology.

Ryann was beginning to understand; at least she had a much more profound understanding than before. Terri closed her eyes and listened to her heartbeat for a moment. It seemed to keep the slow, soothing pace of Ryann's back rub rhythm.

"Why wouldn't a family member just go grab her from the house?" Ryann asked what would keep the family from visiting.

"Sometimes they move, and the victims won't tell anyone where. They call and talk to family and friends, but never give specific information, at least not enough information for them to be found. The victims don't want to face possible consequences of telling anyone where they were, just in case someone did show up. They live daily with the threat of losing everything if they do."

"Do you think he would actually kill her or her family?" She wanted to know.

"He could. It depends. One never knows what these guys are thinking."

"So he is a registered sex offender already, right? Can't you guys go over to his house and check his address? Hopefully, he won't be there, then you can arrest him on that charge and get him away from her," Ryann suggested as she scratched Terri's back in playful circles.

"We will be doing that, but tomorrow David and I have to head to a training seminar. We will be gone most of the day, so it will have to wait. He is registered at an address in town though, off Watson, I think. We will be checking to see if he is there. Arresting him is a more complicated matter though. We will definitely check it."

"You know, what?" Terri asked, "I have to drop Duke off in the morning, and we have better things to talk about," she had absolutely no remorse for her early afternoon excursion with Allison, "Let's go inside."

Chapter 14

It was early in the afternoon, and Ryann figured it was the perfect time to be out snooping around. Terri and Cooper had gone to a police-training seminar about conducting crime scene evaluations. It was in a neighboring town, and they would not be back until later in the evening.

Although both had significant training in the past, the opportunities to use their knowledge had been limited to a few busted roadside mailboxes, until now.

She parked her car in the Meijer parking lot, very close to the run-down Dodge and an old Ford that had been clearly parked for some time. She hopped out and headed to the store.

She milled around casually making her way from one end of the store to the other. She searched and filtered through every rack while scoping out the overhead security camera locations. She only noticed four and wondered if they were on or even worked.

She purchased an iced tea and exited the store, heading toward her vehicle. She walked right by it and onto the sidewalk that led past Monica Street to Fitzpatrick. *What a beautiful day for walking, and the sun is shining. I hope I don't run into anyone walking their dog or bicycling. This town is so small,* she thought.

Ryann walked past the intended target house and knocked on the neighbor's door. *No answer.* The next home was too far down the block, and the only other house with any sort of view was directly across the street. That house was vacant with a 'For Sale' sign in the front lawn.

A row of carefully planted pine trees camouflaged the target house on the other side. A row of bushes had been planted in the back, though they were not tall enough to become a makeshift fence. The house directly behind on Division was also for sale, and the backyards blended somewhere in the middle.

She debated whether to cross the street and opted not to. It was eerily quiet as she bent under the long arching pine branches and made her way to the rear door of the target house. She was completely invisible to the public.

Ryann already knew there would not be animals in the house, so she wasn't concerned with a possible canine alarm. She did not waste any more time than caution allowed as she turned the knob preparing for it to be locked. The doorknob turned completely in her hand. *Great, there must be a deadbolt. Damn it.* She was prepared for the lock, not the deadbolt. She leaned into the door to test its strength and possibly look for a weak point in the door. Most deadbolts were near the top of the door, but some had two, one on each end. Surprisingly, the door eased open with minimal effort.

Are you serious, right now? She asked herself in disbelief. The door was not locked. *Could it be that he was home? Or maybe he just forgot to lock it?* Her anxiety was steadily increasing; she was trapped between shutting the door and running or yelling inside to pretend her opening the door was somehow an honest mistake.

"Hello?" Ryann spoke softly at first, "Hello?"

She entered the door and stood halfway in and repeated significantly louder, "Hello?" *Not a sound, not even an echo from the house.* Ryann closed the door behind her; she was standing in the kitchen. It was dull and dreary. The place was as she imagined with layers of dust coating the microwave, kitchen plants, and even the utensils standing in a jar.

Her eyes caught a picture hanging from the stainless steel refrigerator with a palm tree magnet. "I'm here for you," Ryann mumbled staring at the picture.

She felt her skin grow warm and her eyes begin

to water. She was staring at a near image of herself. The hair was similar and styled the same; the eyes were perfect reflections of their parents. They were the same height and weighed the same.

Ryann had given her all of her hand-me down clothes and they shared jackets and jeans until Rebecca moved out of her family's home and married David.

Standing in the same room together, their infectious smiles and laughter made visitors, and even family believe they were twins. Behind closed doors, it was nearly impossible to tell which one was talking.

Ryann made her way out of the kitchen and headed straight for the hallway in search of David's home office and bedroom. His bedroom was meticulous. *Creepy.* The bedroom was the only really clean room in the house. The bed was made without a single crease; the pillowcase was smooth across the top.

On his dresser was an old wind-up clock, a small hand-carved woman's jewelry box that she assumed belonged to Rebecca at one point, and a vanilla candle.

Ryann opened the jewelry box out of curiosity. *Yes, it did belong to Rebecca, or at least it must have. This is definitely woman's jewelry, the type she would have worn. Wait, wait a minute.* Ryann pulled a short, thin necklace with ballerina charm attached. *This is the one I mailed to Hayley for her third birthday.* Nauseating feelings flooded her stomach, and she felt herself grow pale. She closed the lid and held onto the box; she made mental notes along with her search.

She opened the top drawer and found David's underwear, a spare semi-automatic pistol, porn magazines, a few unmarked recordable CD's, an address book, and a few hundred dollars folded into a sock. Ryann snapped a few pictures with her cell phone and picked up the address book.

She started flipping the pages, but stopped at the third flip; she could not believe her eyes. A photograph was stapled to the top of each page along with a name, an email address, and a physical home address. She stood in total disbelief.

She wanted so desperately to have her feelings validated that she did not think to prepare herself if she was right. Ryann was staring at young girls, very young. Perhaps aged 7 to 10 years old.

In fact, every page of the address book held a photograph and what appeared to be a text-chat name and email address. Her suspicions about David were suddenly confirmed, and she knew now that David had raped her sister and had probably been sexually abusing his own daughter. She took several pictures of the open pages and placed the address book back in the drawer where she had found it.

Ryann sat on the bed, recalling why her sister married David. Rebecca was pregnant with his baby. She had just turned 16 and was excitedly in love, with him. He was 28, a full 13-year difference. She recalled how it made their father intensely mad and her mother unforgiving. David was not allowed into the house, and Rebecca felt she had no choice but to run away with him.

Eventually, Rebecca called home. It was just before baby Hayley was born. Since then, and right up to the crash, Rebecca and her mother had a close telephone and texting relationship, but David would not let them come to his house. Mom and dad would not forgive him, and her father would not allow David at his house either.

She and mom had secretly met Rebecca and Hayley on many occasions. Even then it was for a very limited amount of time. The last time she saw her was two weeks before the fatal crash that killed her. They talked about her escape from David and Rebecca had said she was ready to leave.

Rebecca told her she thought he was molesting their daughter and she did not want to stand by while he did it, but she was afraid and confused. David had always told her he loved them, loved them both equally. Not to mention David was a police officer and always threatened that he would kill all of them if she ever told anyone. He told her he would not lose his career over her lies. And she would not dare leave him; that would only embarrass him. Ryann struggled to hold back tears.

Together, she and Rebecca were going to come up with a plan for her escape. Her emotions were bound up and they reached across her neck with tightening fingers. Her only sister and niece consumed in a senseless, seemingly premeditated crash.

Ryann grabbed the CD's and headed for David's home office. She found his laptop in the usual place. She flipped it open and the screen lit up. *Dumbass, you left it on!* Ryann was thankful she didn't have to try to get through a sequence of passwords, although she was completely capable.

The screen saver was a series of running photographs. They were all young girls, some barely dressed. Their trusting and unknowing smiles captured in still frame after still frame. She stood in disgust, disbelief, and her knees weak with anger. She snapped another photo of the laptop and then several of the crossing screensavers. *Proof, if I should ever need it. David you are a sick.*

She placed the CD into the drive, and once the computer recognized the device, an auto-play dialog box appeared mid-screen. She chose the 'Open Folder' option to view the files. Immediately, another dialog box appeared requesting action for Windows to open picture files stored on the CD. She double clicked the first folder icon, and the screen provided a listing of more than 200 photograph icons. Selecting the first one, she was horrified. *Pornographic Photos of Children! Bastard.*

She stopped the CD and hit eject. She wanted to crush it into a million tiny bits and leave it scattered on the floor, but she shoved it in her backpack instead. She took two other CD's and replaced them with blanks. *I will take these too, just in case.*

His home office housed his police gear. Uniforms were hung in the closet neatly. His riot gear, radios, evidence collection kits, and mounds of paper from work.

She noticed a red folder with a bright yellow label, 'Dragon Slayers.'

"This must be your new past time, your 'gamer' club Terri is always talking about," she said to herself. Opening the folder, she saw an agenda of some sort, past dates and times with locations.

She found herself reading the group names; Team 2 Square, Avengers until Death, Dragon Slayers. *What is this?* She thought. Thumbing through the pages, she saw the real confirmation she had gone there to see.

There were club member names, meeting dates and times, and each 'player' had been assigned a challenge. *Holy fuck,* she thought.

Each of these players was assigned a text-chat name. She returned to the bedroom drawer and compared the photographs to the players. *Each player was assigned a child! You sick fuck, you are the ringleader of a complicated scheme of child pornography and worse! I can't believe this is true, but it is. No longer you bastard, no longer.* She made a solemn vow his hauntings would end soon.

Her phone alarm chimed in a reminder of the time, and she realized her welcome had been overstayed. She had taken the necessary photographs and documented the evidence; she left the same way she arrived. It was still mid-afternoon, and it would be at least a couple of hours before Terri and David were done with training.

There was plenty of time for her to walk back to Meijer and get her car. She would be long gone, and the engine would have time to cool in the driveway if Terri decided to stop over.

Chapter 15

Terri was near Stern Creek Road on her way back to the office when the cymbals from her phone clashed. "Hello, this is Terri?" She said into the receiver.

"Hello?" There was a long pause on the other end.

"Terri? This is Allison. Do you think we could meet tonight?"

Terri looked down at her watch, *8:15 pm, damn. I've been gone all day, and I don't think Ryann will be over, I could call her and find out though.* She was rationalizing a means to meet her.

"Do you think I could get with you before I get out of work? Like in 30 minutes or so?" Terri asked, not wanting to be late getting home from work tonight, Ryann was already beginning to distance herself in the relationship.

"I just finished a run, and I'm hitting the shower. That sounds good to me," Allison stated. "Is it alright if we met by that curve on Stern Creek Road?" She asked.

"Stern Creek? I'm not too far from there now. Is it important, you sound bothered?" Terri suddenly remembered Allison had something to ask her. She had mentioned it last week when they had breakfast.

"Could we meet at that cemetery about a mile from there? I just have a few questions about this curve, and maybe if we drove down there together, I could explain better. And, Terri, from what I've heard, you are the person that would have the most information about it."

"What you've heard?" Terri asked.

"You've been on the road the longest and taken a

few crashes on this curve. Can we talk about it when you get here?" Allison asked.

"I will be there," she told her as she turned off Highway 612 and began the drive to the cemetery.

Ryann won't know who I might meet up with while I'm at work, who would tell her anyway? The cemetery. Such an eerie place, but desolate, she thought. *I bet she just wants to meet me here where it is quiet and we can be alone.*

The sound of cymbals clashed from the cup holder in the patrol vehicle. She absent-mindedly answered, "I'm on my way" as she looked at her watch, it would take her about 5 minutes to get to Stern Creek Cemetery.

"Terri?" Ryann asked.

"Oh, hey...I'm sorry I thought you were someone else," she stuttered as she spoke, scrambling for an excuse.

"Hi, I was just checking in any way, I know you have been busy. Want me to head to your place and let Duke out?" She asked.

"No, Duke is not with me, I left him a Trisha' for the day because I went to training, remember? But I am actually on my way to pick him up," she told her.

"Great! So I will meet you at your place?" Ryann wanted to see her and ask about the training.

"No, I have to pick him up for a canine call. I just got a call for a track that will probably keep me out late tonight," she lied. *Just like any other night when I worked late. She has no way of knowing.*

"That's okay. Maybe I'll just head to your place and wait? I can keep the beer on ice if you want?"

"Sure, honey, of course. I just don't think I'll be home much before midnight or one," she caught herself trying to get Ryann off the phone.

"I know work has been hectic lately and you are working on those cases. I'll just go to my place. Could you call me when you are on your way home, so I know you are okay? You know how I worry about you," Ryann asked her.

Terri sensed Ryann's frustration at the lack of communication, but she was too busy and didn't always have time for the small details that a real relationship would require.

"Yes, dear. I'll call you. I have to go, I'll talk to you tonight," Terri hung up as she rolled to a stop near the cemetery entrance.

Stern Creek Cemetery was at least 150 years old; marked headstones pre-dated the civil war. It was an astonishing place to be on a clear fall night. The moon casted rays through the trees that lined the drive. The temperature had dropped enough to exhale a mist of visible air. Terri's headlights centered on a figure standing near the shoulder.

Allison was standing on the path, waiting. *Damn, she is hot.* Her thoughts drifted as she saw Allison wrapped in a thin long black coat, she was holding a briefcase.

The coat complimented her figure nicely. She stood shivering until Terri pulled close enough so she could open the door.

"Get in. You must be freezing?" Terri said, "Why are you waiting outside and where did you park your car?"

"There isn't much room in this patrol car is there?" Allison asked nervously, ignoring the questions. Terri noticed she wasn't wearing much to keep her warm, so she leaned over and cranked the heat up.

"Oh, where is your dog? Is that where he stays?" She asked about the empty back seat. It was hard plastic with metal racks; it appeared to be an oversized kennel.

"Yes, that is where he usually stays. I had training today, and he couldn't stay home by himself. I wasn't sure what time I would be back, and it would have been a long day for him locked up without eating or going to the bathroom," Terri made it sound as if she were single and there was no one to help her take care of him when she was gone.

"I have a couple of questions, it won't take too long, but maybe we could drive down to the curve on Stern Creek?" Allison asked.

She drove up the winding path through the cemetery toward the ridge that overlooked Stern Creek; she paused the truck for the view before turning around.

"Wow. What a breathtaking view and look at that low set moon just cresting the trees. Of all the moon phases, it is the early moon I find so amazing, don't you?" Allison asked.

Terri was already beginning to sweat, and she couldn't tell if it was the heat in vehicle or her own nervousness.

The truck was still stopped and Terri was contemplating her next move when Allison reached for her.

"I wanted to see you. I wanted to ask you some questions about someone you may know," Allison began rubbing Terri's leg as she spoke, almost as if she were rubbing her own leg to warm up.

"What is it? It sounded important," Terri began to ask as she lifted herself from the seat, leaning across the in-car radios. She pushed her face toward Terri's and pressed her lips flatly against her mouth.

Terri felt them soft and cold, and then she opened her mouth, her tongue was piercingly warm as she seductively kissed her.

"Perhaps we should get more comfortable?" Allison suggested as she unzipped her coat to reveal a sleek, sexy lacy bra, "Truthfully, I can't keep my mind off you. I can't help but to kiss you; I think about you all of the time."

"I thought you wanted to talk about something. Didn't you say you needed information about someone I knew? I see you are not wearing a shirt..." Terri tried to pull her eyes from the firm rounded breasts beckoning for her to touch them from the other side of the car.

Before getting lost in the next inevitable move, Terri gave an earnest attempt at making sure the dispatcher would not interrupt them. She snapped up the hand mic, "3742, I'll be 102. I'll advise when I am clear."

Terri gave dispatch the code for 'bathroom break,' or 'follow up' and 'don't bother me until I'm done' to dispatch. She flipped her portable shoulder radio off as Allison grabbed onto the antenna and pulled it from her uniform. Their mouths were meeting in hungered passion, Allison was busy working the buttons on Terri's uniform.

Their tongues embraced as Terri pushed her coat from her shoulders. Then she tugged her bra strap down, her skin smooth as silk. She tucked her mouth into her neck and breathed the soft scent of perfume.

Allison left the coat on her seat as she climbed over to release the back of Terri's seat, causing it to fall slightly backward. She was instantly thankful that Duke's cage was not hindering movement.

She struggled a little with Terri's shirt until she realized her gun belt was in the way, "How do I get this off?" Allison whispered as she tugged at the belt around Terri's waist.

"How about this too? Help me with the velcro straps that hold your bulletproof vest together," Terri's duty gear and uniform were providing a protective outer shell that Allison viewed as a challenge.

Terri slipped an arm out of her shirt, still tucked in at the waist where the belt was hooked. She tugged one Velcro shoulder strap down, releasing the right side of the vest. Instantly Allison's hand was moving across her t-shirt and onto her breast, messaging first then rubbing harder.

"We really shouldn't be here, doing this," Terri's words fell like paper in the breeze as Allison pulled herself over the center radio console, clicking the radio "off" and the siren on. RRRRRRRRRRR...the siren yelped into the night air. Terri reached over instinctively and turned the siren off.

Allison took full advantage of Terri's willingness to participate in the performance, "Take this off," she pleaded, pulling at the belt clip.

"No. Not yet, I can't," Terri whispered. Unfortunately, the seat did not only allow Allison to climb over to her side.

Terri imagined her petite, shapely legs resting in a crouched position on either side of Terri.

She was holding her arms and had her hand on the back of her neck, working her fingers into the muscles and moving upward and back down to her shoulders.

Allison leaned forward and wedged her mouth into Terri's neck, sucking softly and intently, pushing her tongue into the sensitive muscle that made Terri achingly wet.

Allison's knee hit the emergency button on the radio, and the dispatcher broke the intensity, "3742 status check?"

Allison kissed her hard on the mouth, distracting her for the moment, and then Terri snapped back to reality, "Hold on a second. Be very quiet," she told Allison. "Dispatch 3742. I'm clear and available," she responded.

"3742 can you call dispatch?"

"Stand by one. Now you must be very quiet while I make this call," Terri told Allison as she moved from her crouched position and sat back in the passenger seat.

She dialed the numbers and waited for the answer, "Dispatch, it is Terri. You asked me to call?" She tried to sound like she really would take another run at this moment.

"Nothing holding. Are you out of service now?" Dispatch asked, hoping she would take herself home so he wouldn't have to worry about her anymore this evening.

"Yes, you can take me off the board. I will be on the way shortly," Terri gave him the signal that she wouldn't be doing any more this evening unless it was an absolute emergency.

She turned to Allison and pulled herself together, "Did you just want to see me, or was there something else?"

"Honestly, this was a nice surprise. But I did have a question, and since you asked...can we drive down to the Stern Creek curve?" Allison asked, straightening her hair.

"Maybe we should just pick up where we have left off," Terri suggested, wondering if they could simply stay parked in the patrol car for another thirty minutes.

"No, no. I can't. I have some important calls to make this evening, and it is already getting late," Allison hesitated just enough to make Terri believe she might be playing hard to get.

Terri was convinced; those beautiful blue eyes and dazzling white smile made her feel wanted. For the first time, Terri was starting to feel guilty, but that quickly faded as she remembered Ryann would not be expecting her for a while, so she felt safe.

"Okay, then. Let's drive down and see if we can't get you what you need," Terri put the vehicle in drive and headed to the curve. Eleven. Wow. Sure doesn't feel like eleven, she noticed the time.

Allison's phone buzzed a quick hissing sound. She didn't look, rather pointed down toward the curve as they drew near, "There." She pointed to a curve marker, a metal attenuator post.

"What?" Terri stopped the vehicle and they both got out.

"Well, I was looking for this marker, see the little green square attached to the steel?" Allison pointed to a green metal sign. It was no larger than a dollar bill.

"Yes, it says 035D. What does that mean?"

"Well, it is a curve marker, and it indicates the number of turns on this road, as well as the proposed speed. See that is green?" Allison was pulling out crash reconstruction knowledge that Terri was not well versed in.

"I'm looking for something different. Let me know if you see a white post, like a round tube; it will have a color painted on the top," Allison needed Terri to find it.

Terri took out her flashlight and waved it across

the ditch. Spotting a white reflective post with blue tags toward the top, "Like this one?"

"Yes, exactly. That is what I was hoping to see," Allison began walking toward it.

"Wait. What were you hoping to see?" Terri wanted to know. She followed close behind.

"Do you see any others?" Allison asked her to survey the rest of the area while they walked.

"No. Not one. What does that mean? And what was your question?"

Allison took a deep breath and asked her question, "Does this area ever flood? You know, like in the spring?" She waved her hand toward the creek.

"Yes, every spring it does, and sometimes in the summer if the rains are heavy enough. Is that your question?" Terri did not understand.

"Yes, that was my question. You see this PVC pipe sticking up with this blue label means it is a water pipe. There are water pipes lining this field and most likely drain tile. And it makes sense, too, because of the overflow from the creek. You would want to keep clean water clean, and the unfiltered dirty water headed back to the creek where it belonged. We should see drain markers somewhere. There- over by the road, do you see it?"

"My claims adjustment team was having a difficult time settling an important complaint. It seems this whole area is a flood zone," Allison stretched the truth. "It makes sense to me now, and this complaint can be closed," she told her.

They walked back to the truck, Terri was still thinking. They climbed back in and Terri asked, "What was the claim?"

"Well, a complainant intended to file suit against the county and his vehicle insurer, due to a struck gas pipeline in this area. You could say we have just 'blown' that theory out of the 'water' since there are no other utility markers in the area- not for miles!" Allison was pleased with the research she had previously completed at the local library of the land surveys.

"So, you were looking for gas pipelines?" Terri asked.

"Yes, I am quite relieved honestly, it was a wealthy policy if you know what I mean. My company is off the hook," Allison let her know it would be one claim not satisfied.

Terri didn't immediately get the reference, but the seed had been planted.

"Great! Another case completed! Does that mean you are done here in Waterford?" She wanted one night with her. She was hoping Ryann would not be at her house, if only for this one evening.

Terri did not give her time to answer. Instead, she cut right to the chase, "Why don't' we go somewhere for a little bit? Like, you are staying at the Hampton, right?"

"No. I can't," Allison said firmly.

Defeated, Terri drove them back to Stern Creek cemetery and parked upon the hill. *That was all she wanted? She wanted to ask me if the road flooded? She did say she wanted my help, but maybe she just wanted to spend time with me.* Terri reasoned as Allison gathered herself and zipped her coat. She kissed Terri again and exited the vehicle, "Thank you."

Terri watched as she walked through the silhouetted trees and disappeared.

Allison reached the hotel and sat at the room office table while she situated her notes. She decided sitting on the bed would be a more comfortable place to speak from and transitioned over before making her call. She dialed the number and waited for an answer.

"Mrs. Kisne, please," after a few moments Allison began talking again.

"Hi, Mrs. Kisne. Of course, I'm doing well. No, I already talked it over with Christine and..." Allison was interrupted mid-sentence.

"Let me get to that, yes," she told Mrs. Kisne.

"Okay, well, the first answer is 'yes.' I was on the road near that intersection. I spent significant time out there, and I rented a vehicle to test the road surface. So, yes. Yes it was possible to lose control and drive off the road in that same area. But, at the same time, it was nearly impossible to roll the vehicle. It would have to have been intentionally driven along the edge, and even then someone would have had to crank the steering wheel to point the tires down the embankment," she explained.

Allison continued, "I tried several times. Eventually, I drove it straight in, all the way to the creek. Even when I tried to get straight over the embankment, it would not roll," she was speaking slowly and clearly.

"That's exactly right. It did. Nope, each time I was able to slow down enough after I left the road, and before getting to the creek to turn and drive out." Allison explained how she had tested the road surface for stopping and turning. She also explained how she had driven into the weeded area before the creek and successfully maneuvered the vehicle back to the roadway to try again.

She was listening intently to Mrs. Kisne and then she answered, "I agree. It certainly seems that someone proficient at driving, and familiar with the area would have either slowed down or driven out of the thickets before reaching the creek." Allison flipped through the notes she had taken about that particular corner of the road.

"Mrs. Kisne, hold on a second. Yes, I know. No, I did the measurements, and I am certain that it happened that way. There could not have been any real braking. None. That's right. Yes, it does appear to have been driven to the edge and stopped along the embankment, then left to roll over with the wheels turned. I understand what that means. Do you need a minute? It's okay, pull yourself together, that's why we are here, remember? Let me call you back in a few minutes. Go get something to drink, and I'll call you back." Allison was patient and didn't want to overload her with all of the information at once.

She was nervous as she opened the refrigerator and took out a cold beer. She needed to finish the discussion with Mrs. Kisne. It was one of the more difficult conversations she had ever had. She called her back after a small sip.

"Mrs. Kisne, are you okay?" She asked, "I spent a lot of time at the library where they have a couple of private rooms. I confirmed with microfilm the previous construction tests on the road, and the reported traffic incidents at that location. The speed division of the National Traffic Safety Association approved the posted limits, and the city confirmed the reduced speed sign control at a public hearing about five years ago." Allison had been doing her homework, "For the crash report to have made sense, she must have been driving at least 50 miles an hour over the speed limit. Yes, Mrs. Kisne, 50. 50 miles per hour *over* the limit. Yes, around 75 or 80."

"Ok, now lastly..." she was interrupted with more questions. "Yes, I talked to Christine already. She did the investigation on that part. She was at the house and confirmed our suspicions. Do you want to hear it from her?" Allison was only making sure she was settled down enough to listen to the results.

"Ok, I don't have all the details, but yes. She was at his house. I think you should call her tomorrow, it is already too late tonight," Allison was thankful she would not have to explain any further. Hearing it from Christine would be difficult enough.

"Well, I'm not going into details, not now. You can talk to Christine tomorrow," Allison didn't have the heart. It was obvious the information had already emotionally shaken Mrs. Kisne.

"Yes, I think it is enough. It is more than enough Mrs. Kisne. Once you talk to Christine, I think you will have verification of what you already suspected. What you already believed was completely true."

Allison was convinced, "I believe it is true. I have no doubt. We have no doubt." She flipped to the last page of her notes and recapped the information in her mind.

"Christine has been careful. No, she has been calling the officer to check her locations. Yes, she is able to keep track because of the GPS on her phone. She seems to be very naive about what has been happening," Allison explained how they have been able to work around Terri.

"That will all be taken care of Mrs. Kisne. Yes, accountability and responsibility. Yes, he will be held to both. I will talk to Christine and let her know you are calling. I have some other business to take care of first," Allison knew she would have to meet with Terri at least one more time before she could leave.

"Love you, too. See you in a few days," the call was disconnected. Allison gathered her things and tidied the room one last time and packed for home.

Chapter 16

"Morning, Jack," Terri said as she came in the side door. She was feeling a little tired from the late evening. He was standing with his back against the wall trying to peel the plastic cover from some nasty cheap microwave breakfast.

"I don't know how you eat that stuff," she commented.

"Well, the Mrs. cooks wonderfully, but not in the morning before she has had a chance to have a cup of coffee or two," Jack replied with a smile. "At least this is better than the breakfast burrito I am used to eating." He had a dry sense of humor.

The office phones began to ring; it was almost 8 a.m. "I'll get it, Jack," Terri yelled down the hall as she walked to the front office, "Waterford City Police."

"Detective Bradford, please, "The voice crackled on the other end.

"Speaking," Terri replied.

"Ahem, sorry about that, I didn't expect an answer so quickly, and I choked on my coffee!" The voice apologized for coughing into the receiver then continued to clear her throat.

"This is Dr. Anderson from the County Coroner's office. I wanted to speak with the lead investigator in the Moore matter." The coroner was professional and direct.

"That would be me. Do you want me to head to your office, or is it something we can discuss on the phone?" Terri said excitedly.

"I think you should come down to the office; I have a couple of things I would like to show you. I think you may find them interesting, at least I do," Dr. Anderson urged.

"Absolutely! I need a few minutes here, and I will be on my way! I will be over around 10:00 am. Will that work?" Terri was calculating drive time to Havelock.

"I do not have time in my schedule this morning because I have two in from last night. I won't have time until noon, can we meet then?"

"Yes, ma'am. I will be there, and thank you," Terri said.

"What's that all about?" Jack had made his way down the hall with his warmed up microwave breakfast.

"It was the coroner on my other case. She wanted to discuss it, so I'm going to head to Havelock. Well, as long as the guys don't mind covering the shift."

"You mean Jones and Reese? Those guys are always ready to help. Now, Cooper? That's a different story," Jack took a bite of food.

"Have you heard from him today? He is usually here by now," it was always like Cooper to be on his own schedule, especially when something important came up.

"If he isn't here by the time I leave I will call him. He was probably out late with his 'game club' again," she speculated.

"If that's what you call it. I call it a waste of time and a waste of mind," he smiled at Terri and ate the last of his breakfast.

Terri walked back to the detective cubicles and found Jones at his desk.

"Hey, Randy. You must have snuck in the back door. I'm glad you are here though; there's something about this case that's been bothering me. Do you think you could look into it so I can get these reports tightened up? Or maybe you could see if Pierce has time to check up on it. If not, maybe you could ask Jessica," she asked.

"Sure, Terri. What case is it and what do you want me to ask?" Jones asked.

"Did you have time to check on that receipt we found on the guy in the box? The one from Meijer?" Terri asked.

"In fact, I have that right now. I was just looking over the email Meijer security sent me, and they have parking lot video to from the date and time of the receipt,"

Jones told her.

He read through the email and sent the PDF file to the printer, "Just printed it, Terri, let's see what it says."

Jones pulled it off the printer and started reading, "Meijer, item 1, $12.95, stuffed bear, ballerina, item 2 was a gift bag $2.99, Hershey kisses, $3.99, and gummy bears, $1.99, paid in cash."

"Damn, I was hoping for a credit card. Does the surveillance show a person at the register?" She asked.

"Well, it does, but there were birthday balloons blocking the view of that particular register. But the video from the parking lot shows a person driving through the lot and parking at the far end about 15 minutes before," Jones told her.

"Did they send the video file?" Terri wanted to watch it for herself.

"No, but the security manager said he could see someone walking toward the east end of the parking lot during that time frame," he said.

"You know what? Why don't you head over there and see if you can run some plates parked on the east end. You know, where all those other vehicles are parked," Terri asked.

"The ones for sale?"

"Yeah, the ones left under the street lights," Terri gave him a task.

"Ok, ma'am. I am on it," Jones gathered his files on Moore and Kramer, "I'll look for the vehicles listed on their registry information."

"Sounds good. I have to head up to Havelock to meet with the County Coroner. She called this morning and wanted to meet for a few minutes. She had something she wanted to show me."

"On our case?" Jones asked.

"She said something about Moore, but she did not get into details on the phone. I will be back this afternoon. Need anything before I leave?" Terri locked up her desk drawer and headed for the door.

"All set. Let me know if you need anything."

"Morning, honey," Terri called Ryann on her way to Havelock, "I'm going to be in Havelock most of the afternoon," there was a hint of excitement in her voice.

"What for?" Ryann asked.

"I have to meet with the medical examiner about one of our cases. I hope she has some good information for me," Terri stated.

"Is your partner going with you?"

"David? No, no. He hasn't shown up for work yet. He is probably still sleeping," Terri sounded irritated.

"It's better he doesn't go with me. It gives me time to ask some questions without acting like we already know everything," Terri didn't fully appreciate David's haughty omniscient attitude. "I'll call you later; maybe we can have dinner tonight if you are free?" Terri suggested.

"If I'm available? It's your schedule that we are always trying to work around," Ryann sounded disinterested.

"What is that supposed to mean?" Terri raised her voice.

"Well, you seem to be so tied up with work all the time that I don't think you know how to sit down or go out and enjoy dinner. I'm not saying I don't want to go out with you, but don't make promises you can't keep," Ryann condemned.

"I'm sorry, dear. You know these cases we have, I can't just let them go," Terri was trying to blame work for her transgressions, but she knew she had spent more time thinking about Allison than focusing on either one of the murders.

"If you think about it you can call me when you get a chance," Ryann sounded sincere but not hopeful.

Terri rolled into the medical examiner's office parking lot and found a vacant spot near the door. She brushed the crumbs from her bagel off her lap and picked up her now nearly cold coffee. She walked halfway to the door before stopping and turning back. She had forgotten to lock the car. *I almost forgot. I get so comfortable in my little town.*

Terri entered the building and was greeted by the reception staff, "You must be Detective Bradford, Waterford PD?" The young lady behind the counter looked like an intern and couldn't be more than 17 years old, Terri guessed.

"Yes, I have an appointment with Dr. Anderson."

"Alright, just sign in, please. I will let her know you are here. She is finishing up right now," the intern left the room and Terri found a chair.

This is probably the hardest chair in the room. She stood up to move, but Dr. Anderson was already at the side door inviting her in.

"Detective Bradford? Dr. Anderson. Come in please." Dr. Anderson reached forward to shake Terri's hand.

"Just call me Terri, Doc. No need for formalities."

"Ok, Terri. Let's go down to the conference room. I have a few images I would like you to see. I took them using projection radiography. I think you might find them interesting, if not pertinent to your investigation."

Dr. Anderson walked quickly down the hall toward the conference room. Terri followed, and they were soon inside a small room where two x-ray films were already in place on a set of wall mounted light boxes.

"I wanted to show you the x-rays of the victims, and you will see why in just a minute."

Dr. Anderson pointed to the first set of x-rays and started to explain, "Bone is very dense, and it processes on the radiographs as a white color. The lungs are mostly air, and they will show up more black."

"Okay, I get it," Terri eased herself into a conference room chair, "I see the full lungs, and the rib cage is laced in white, the strips of bone."

"Yes, I wanted to go over the pictures of your two victims first, then show you another set," Dr. Anderson pointed to the first one hanging on the left.

"This is a lateral side of the skull, and it appears

normal. This one is of the neck, and so is the second one. The vertebras at the top of the neck, these ones," Dr. Anderson highlighted the axis area of the neck, "this is where the cranium sits on top of the spine."

"Okay," Terri said, trying to follow along.

"On this frontal view of the neck area, you are supposed to be able to separately identify the larynx, thyroid cartilage, cricoid cartilage, and the cervical vertebras," Dr. Anderson explained.

Dr. Anderson showed Terri a normal radiograph of a heart attack victim. The neck bones were in the appropriate place. "This is what the neck should look like," Dr. Anderson said.

"Now, this one is your guy, Moore," she pointed to the second film.

"Holy Shit! Someone took a big swing at this guy's neck!" Terri blurted, "It looks like a bunch of toothpicks." She commented about the mush of small bones that seemed crumpled together in the middle of the throat.

"Not only that, but every vertebra is moved to the left. The crush indentations are coming from the right side. What stands out to me is the area of the initial impact," Dr. Anderson was drawing a square around the fifth cervical vertebra.

"You can see it's not at the top, which would indicate an upward blow. And it isn't at the base of the neck, so it doesn't indicate a downward blow. The crushing of the neck was nearly a strike swing."

"So, the person was probably a little taller?" Terri pretended she was holding a baseball bat and took a practice swing.

"Maybe. The victim could have been sitting down," Dr. Anderson guessed.

"I thought it was an unlucky freak accident. Like maybe the person didn't mean to kill him. But if you look at the fifth cervical vertebra and where it is damaged, or crushed, such as in this instance, the person would be unable to breathe. The spinal cord nerves run between the fifth and third vertebra. Even if this guy would have survived the crushing blow, he would most likely have been paralyzed from the neck down."

"I see, so this is either a good shot or an unlucky one?" Terri asked.

"I guess that would depend on the intent. I have reason to believe it was a calculated one. The x-rays we just looked at are from the Moore case," Dr. Anderson moved back toward the table and pulled out another radiograph of a neck.

"Now, take a look at this one," she removed the first radiograph and replaced it with another.

"They look the same?" Terri was stunned.

"Yes, this is the radiograph of the murder victim Kramer," she reached into an envelope and pulled out another radiograph.

"Now, there is this one. This is the third one, and I definitely believe it was intentional and premeditated. They all appear to have the same type of crushing injuries in the same location. Neither could have survived, even with immediate intervention..."

"Doctor Anderson, we don't have a third murder. Who is the last guy? What agency brought him in?" Terri did not know what to say.

"We don't know who he is yet. The County Sheriff found him during a sex offender address verification check."

"Another sex offender? What in the hell is going on? We have a killer of sex offenders on the loose? Who is the officer in charge on that case? I have to get ahold of him immediately. Why didn't they call me?" Terri was pissed about not knowing since their cases were so similar.

"Officer Bancroft will be here any minute. I don't blame him for not contacting you right away, though. When they first brought this guy in he was covered in blood. Not like your guys," Dr. Anderson explained.

"Covered in blood? I thought you said his throat was crushed?" Terri asked.

"Yes, it was. But this guy was also was repeatedly stabbed. I found several stab wounds on the guy. None of them were very deep; at least not deep enough to kill him. I believe the throat injury was first though because I didn't find any defensive wounds in his arms or hands. I'm guessing your murderer was angry, and this sure seems personal."

"Shallow wounds?"

"Yes, not enough to puncture organs, but several repeated blows. Maybe a weak person, like a woman," the Coroner suggested.

Terri waited until after her meeting with the County Sheriff's Deputy before she called Jones. She was anxious to get back to Waterford and have a meeting about what she had just learned. The ride was about 45 minutes, but first, she had to stop to fuel up the patrol vehicle and grab a Diet Coke.

"Randy. Hey, it's Terri," she said as he answered. "I've got some news from the medical examiner on our two homicides, and a third murder victim too. I'm planning on having a meeting at the office around 4 o'clock. You need to clear the schedule and be there."

"Yeah, I'm at the front manning the desk. Jack left early today so he I'm sitting in for him. I've got this walk-in bicycle license registration, and then I'm set for the day. Oh, and Jess called me back also, so I can fill everyone in at the meeting as well."

"Ok, when you get a chance, call Mike and have him meet us also, please."

Jones asked, "What time do you think you will be back?"

"I'm on my way right now, shouldn't be but an hour. Oh, wait. Let me call you back, David is buzzing in right now."

Terri switched the line over and answered, "Hello, this is Terri."

"Terri, it's David. Where have you been all

morning? I've been looking for you," he scolded.

"I'm on my way back from the medical examiner. Are you in the office?"

"Yeah, I'm here, but nobody said where you were," Cooper retorted.

"Jones and Reese both knew where I went, did you even ask them?" She knew he probably had not made it to the office yet.

"Yeah, well, uh...I didn't ask them," Cooper lied; he had not been to the office yet.

"Anyway, I have some fascinating information from the medical examiner, and I would like to share it with everyone," Terri began.

"What is it?" Cooper asked.

"I'd rather just have a little conference when I get there. I'm sure it's something the Captain's going to want to know as well. We just might have a serial murderer on our hands," Terri stated.

"What?" Cooper was shocked, "I don't believe it. You haven't told me anything about these cases," his whining was evident.

"David, I've been trying to talk to you but you have not been available. Every time I call you, your phone goes right to voicemail and you don't call me back. I think it is better if we have a small conference and I can share the information with everyone," Terri did not wait for him to respond.

"Since you are at the office, is Randy right there?" She already knew the answer.

"I just stepped out, but when I get back in I will tell him," he lied again. Cooper pouted, "Maybe I won't make it back today. When is your meeting?"

"David, stop acting like such an ass! I'm going to shoot for 4 o'clock so I can tell everyone at the same time. I'm sure everyone will have some ideas about how we should proceed from this point." Terri refused to fill him in before she has had a chance to gather her own thoughts.

"What is it, Terri?" He demanded.

"You will just have to wait. I don't want to repeat it a hundred times," Terri told him.

"Damn it! I'm your partner! You are supposed to be telling me. I should've gone with you this morning," Cooper appealed to her 'brotherhood' side as her neglected partner.

"Well, you know what? You weren't around. I thought you were sleeping in like usual. So don't get on me because I've come to know your habits!" She was condescending and trying not to get angry with Cooper, but now she was driving the patrol vehicle like a demon possessed. She looked at the speedometer and was already 15 miles per hour over the limit.

"David, someone else is ringing in. Let me get back with you. If I don't call you back, I'll see you at the office." Terri hung up and answered, "Hello, this is Terri."

"Terri, it's Pierce. Jarhead said you wanted me to call. He also said you have some pretty decent news from the autopsy."

"Mike, I'm glad you called me back. I am aiming for a meeting at the office at 4 p.m., will you be able to make it?"

"I'm not sure, but if you wait until the morning, I can be there at 10:00 am. Do you think we could postpone it until then?" He had to take his son to a follow-up appointment for his leg and they were already late.

"You know what? David can't make it in either. Let me call Randy and see when works best," she told him and hung up.

"Randy, Terri. A couple of things. First, do you have the list of names you gave Jessica? I was wondering if you could give her a call back and see what kind of information she obtained on that third guy," she asked.

"One step ahead of you. It seems Jeremy Hines was not only an absconding pedophile, but his probation agent busted him with an email address he did not disclose. The Office of Inspector General issued a warrant for him yesterday," Jones started to explain.

"What?" Terri was speechless as she listened.

"The warrant affidavit says he was part of a group known as 2 Squared. You know 2 Squared? That name on the card we found? Jess told me it was an online private group; there might be four participants. She is going to fax the information to me later," Jones told her.

"Terri? Terri? Did you hang up on me?" Jones thought the call dropped.

"No, no. I'm here. Randy, we have a third murder. He was also a sex offender, at least the deputies found him at the registered address of an offender. His neck was crushed in like our two victims. They rolled his prints and are waiting for identification," Terri told him.

"What? Where?" Jones was stunned.

She repeated, "Dr. Anderson did the autopsy on him yesterday. His injuries mimicked Moore and Kramer. Throat punch. With one exception: he was stabbed a bunch of times," she revealed the content of the meeting.

"What agency? Where? Do you think it is Hines? Do they have any clues?" He was full of questions.

"I spoke to County Officer Bancroft about their case. It seems like all the details were like ours, that "2-Squared" card and crushed throat. Except he said, one of his shoes was missing."

"Randy, another Waterford PD business card with David's name on it was in the guy's wallet."

"What, another one? Well, they were registering in Waterford, weren't they?"

"Yes, I suppose you are right," she thought for a few minutes before Jones interrupted with a question.

"So, we are on a shoe hunt? Do you think the killer kept it? You know, a souvenir from his victim?" Jones asked.

"Well, if we find a size ten somewhere, he was missing one," Terri told him. "This is serious Randy; we have to find out if all these guys belonged to the same online group, and if so, we have to find the fourth guy before he is killed."

"A serial killer of pedophiles. Terri, are we going to look for the fourth guy to 'save' him or get him ourselves?" Jones reverted to his training, and he had decided sex offenders, especially pedophiles were the enemy.

"Randy, stop. Call Mike and tell him tomorrow at ten. I will leave a message for David, and I'm about to call the Captain. Are you clear?" Terri gave clear instructions, "We can go over it then."

Terri hung up, her mind racing. She had one more call to make before getting back to the office. She dialed the number and waited.

"Hello?" Ryann answered.

"Hi, babe. I was just thinking about you. I thought I would call and see what you were up to today?" Terri tried to sound sincere.

"Really?" Ryann was skeptical; "I was wondering if you might have time tonight, we could talk about a few things?" Ryann waited for the inevitable excuse.

"That sounds good. But, I am a little tied up at work, maybe we could play it by ear?" Terri suggested.

"How about we just cancel it? The whole idea of meeting this evening," Ryann had enough.

"What?" Terri asked, astonished.

"You always seem to find some excuse not to see me. I wait half the night, take care of your dog, and end up with hurt feelings in the end. It's easier if we don't make plans," Ryann was right.

"If that's the way you want it, then can I call you tonight when I get home?" Terri wasn't sure if she was going to call or not.

"Sure, and if I'm not busy, I will answer," Ryann snapped.

"What's that supposed to mean?"

"Honestly, that is how I feel about my phone calls to you. If you aren't busy, you have time for me. You are never taking the time to put me first," she was trying not to sound upset.

"Ryann, you know I have been very busy at work, and you knew that work was a big part of my life when we met," Terri was defending herself.

She recalled the conversations they had about how Terri didn't have time for a relationship because she was aiming for a promotion at work. She desperately wanted to replace the Captain when it was her turn to run the department. She had sacrificed so much, none the least of which were her personal pleasures.

"I thought you said you were supportive of my career aspirations?" Terri reminded her of the support she once offered.

"Yes, career aspirations. Terri, don't turn this on me. I could have supported your 'career aspirations,' but I wanted to be a part of your life. I did not intend on standing by watching while you lived your life without me."

Terri hung up and did not call her back. *She will call me back.* She was convincing herself when the phone rang.

Ha! She did not look at the cell phone face. Instead, she quickly answered, "Miss me already?"

"Of course…do you want to see me this evening?" The voice was soft and warm.

"Allison? Yes, of course. I will send you my address if you like. Say, tonight around 9?" Terri didn't think twice and quickly texted the street numbers.

Chapter 17

The night air was thin as she walked the back way to his door. She was taking deep meditating breaths. She wasn't anticipating any problems. Putting on her latex kitchen rubber gloves, she let herself in with the key that she had made and shut the door behind her quietly. She felt oddly calm, and although she had been to this place before, tonight it felt different.

The light above the stove was glowing, and it cast small shadows of the salt-and-pepper shakers along the kitchen backsplash. They looked like toy soldiers on the counter, and for a moment she felt they were watching her. Not to be defeated, she pulled off the stove hood-light cover and unscrewed the light bulb, their world now draped in darkness.

From her handbag of tools, she found the flat head screwdriver. She cautiously unscrewed the small rivet holding the kitchen switch plate in place. She placed the switch plate on the counter and removed the receptacle plug. *Don't zap yourself;* she repeated while she loosened the screw on the 'hot' side.

Grasping the black wire on the 200 coated end, she tugged the cable from the housing. Then, very carefully, she bent the flexible wire toward the end of the electrical box and pushed the light switch back into position, leaving it disconnected.

She walked through the kitchen area and into the living room. His house was still incredibly dusty, and she was careful not to touch anything. The pillows on the couch were arranged neatly, and a store bought knitted blanket lay across the back. *I'm surprised there isn't plastic on all his shit.*

The television remote was wedged between the cushions. She sat down for a moment with her bag in her lap and swapped out the screwdriver for a penlight, and then placed the bag on the floor near a dining room chair.

Sifting through the items, she carefully removed one Ziploc plastic baggie. The Ziploc contained one blue cue stick chalk, slightly used, half of a broken pool cue, and a folded paper. She was careful not to handle it too much or get any of the dust on her clothing.

She removed the folded paper and chalk and started down the hallway. She walked to his home office. There was no need to turn lights on, she had been in this room a million times in her head, and she knew where to go and exactly what she was going to do. He was a sick and grotesque man. She never knew what Rebecca had seen in him, but she had finally understood the seduction of her sister.

She used the penlight to find his computer keyboard among the clutter on the desk. She was unfolding the paper she had carried when a reflection caught her eye. The edge of a photograph shimmered in the darkness. She pushed the keyboard out of the way and discovered a folder filled with pictures. She opened it, spreading the contents onto the desk. She was completely horrified. *Why didn't I see these before? Are these new? Jesus Christ, these are new.*

There were more pictures of children, their addresses with personal information written on the back. Oh my God! Is she six maybe? Maybe seven years old? The child was naked except for a teddy bear with purple lace.

An overwhelming warmth flooded into her stomach and she suddenly felt ill. *I think I'm going to throw-up.*

Thumbing through the folder she saw pornographic website lists and there appeared to be chat-room conversations, she couldn't look at anymore. After a few deep breaths, she left the folder and returned the keyboard to its original position.

She placed the chalk down on the corner of the keyboard near the mouse. She picked it back up and just as an extra measure; she rubbed the chalk on a couple of the keys before setting it back in the original position. If anyone were to look at his computer desktop, it would be plain to see. She left the room satisfied that she would be sending the right signal.

She walked from David's office with the folder clutched in her hand. She thrust the folder down upon the kitchen counter in frustration. *You sick fuck.* She exhaled deeply several times, collecting her nerves.

She returned to the living room and sat back down, glancing at the time on her wristwatch. It was only 1030 p.m.; there were still 30 minutes before her plan would go into action. She squeezed her pendant to remain calm. She had the reassurance that someone had her back.

Her adrenaline was pumping with anticipation. Slowly and cautiously she shined the penlight at her feet as she walked to the stairs leading to the basement. She scanned for the light that would illuminate the steps, but there was none. It appeared the stairway was consistently dark if the kitchen or basement lights were not on. *Perfect,* she thought. She walked down the stairs. There were seventeen wooden steps leading from the kitchen to the basement floor.

There was no carpet on the basement floor. There was only a small foot rug lying at the base of the stairs and it matched the one at the top. The cement was cold and dark, painted sealer grey. She used her penlight to find the electric box hanging on the wall. She opened the panel door and found the fuse switch for the kitchen. *Top left.*

She traversed the stairs back to the kitchen. Testing her theory, she pushed the kitchen light switch near the back door to the 'on' position. POP! She switched it back to the 'off' position and returned to the basement, resetting the breaker.

She paused at the top of the stairs to roll the rug into a ball, just enough to trip over.

She rechecked the time, *fifteen minutes.* She scooped up her bag from the floor and sat in the chair. She placed it on her lap and unzipped the top. She pulled out an extra-large Ziploc bag containing one brown Docker, a men's size 10. Brown suede with black hard rubber soles intricate patterns of crisscrosses was molded into the bottom. She placed the bag on the kitchen table while she untied the shoe.

She called Terri if only to offer herself an alibi. To her surprise, the phone rang directly to voicemail, so she left a small message. "Hi, Terri it's me. I'm at your house, sitting in the driveway. I was just wondering if you were coming home tonight? I want to talk to you about this job offer I received and grab the sweatshirt I had left here, but it appears you're busy at work. Call me when you get a chance, thanks."

She pressed the power button on her phone until it was off. "I can't have you ringing or vibrating at an inopportune moment," she said to the phone and tucked it into her purse.

She removed the last item from the bottom of her bag- a collapsible baton she had 'borrowed' from Terri. Terri kept her extra police gear in a bedroom closet. She could have worn a bullet-resistant vest, grabbed handcuffs, and a Taser, but she only needed the baton.

She swung it open in the most extended position. The device had a span of two feet, with the last foot solid steel. There she waited quietly, patiently, until she saw the headlights. Her eyes had adjusted entirely to the dark when she saw them flash across the curtains and stare down the garage.

He stopped short of the overhead door and turned the car off. She played in her mind the minutes it would take for him to enter the door; she could see him now- he was taking out the keys from the ignition, removing his seatbelt if he actually wore one. She imagined he was opening the car door- sliding his left leg out, then the right. Closing the door behind him, he would have 15 paces to the back door.

Counting as he walked, she could hear the doorknob turn. He entered through the garage/kitchen door just as she had expected. Reaching for the kitchen light switch, he flipped it to the 'on' position. "POP!" The disconnected wires resting against the interior of the metal safety plug box did what it was designed to do. It kicked the circuit breaker 'off,' preventing the flow of power and leaving him in total darkness.

"Damn it!" David Cooper murmured. He dropped his car keys on the counter as he made his way to the basement stairs. Her heart pounded so loudly she felt he would hear it. She held her breath. He stumbled on the rug before getting to the stairs, just enough for him to lean over to adjust his footing and catch himself.

She stepped from the shadows and swung as hard as she could, the baton struck David's head with a near-perfect landing. The hardened steel crushed into the back of his skull just beneath the cranium, not too hard, but enough. His body lurched forward, headfirst. He dropped to his knees and picked his head upward gasping.

This time she took a swing to his throat. CRUNCH! The sound of his windpipe sinking into his neck echoed down the stairs. He fell headfirst into the stairway leading to the basement. She strained to see in the blackness, listening to his body strike the stairs and sidewalls. The calamity stopped, and she felt he was finally at the base.

"You stupid mother-fucker," gritting her teeth as she spoke. The anger she had bottled up beginning to find a way to the surface. She wanted to scream at him down the steps.

She pulled out her penlight and walked down to him. The back of his head was bleeding. His nose may have been broken, and there was substantial red blood flowing from it. His arm lay in an awkward, unnatural bent position; the other one lay beneath him.

"Good. You are a total asshole," she managed to say in a much more calm tone.

She walked around his body to inspect his position watching his chest rise and fall, very slowly. Reaching down with one hand, she felt for a pulse on the side of his neck. He was still alive. She grabbed the hair on his head and twisted his face toward her. His eyes rolled open, as he mouthed the words, "help me."

"What? What did you say?" She asked him, drawing her ear closer to his mouth.

"Auuuggghh, (gurgle) I, I, I..." his voice barely audible, he strained to breathe. His nose nearly filled with blood now.

"Aww, what's the matter, David?" He was coughing and choking.

"Let me help you, just be a good boy now," she pushed his head away from her to the wall and, still holding a handful of hair, she tucked his head down as far as it would go.

"David, David, David. I wonder what my sister found out about you, what secret you could have had that made you want to silence her? What's that?" She was mocking him; he couldn't speak.

He would not have told her even if he could.

"She caught you looking at all those poor, little defenseless children? Is that it?" She reminded him of his desktop running portfolio of young girls.

"What's that? David, you want to confess to something? You do?"

Again she used his hair to nod his head up and down, "You want to tell me how you took advantage of my sister? How you raped her? Then you killed her?"

David's eyes were telling the story. His nostrils flared, and eyes were bulging. She knew that he recognized her.

"You want to tell me how my sister caught you raping her daughter? Your own daughter?" Her eyes burned with fury.

He tried pushing his hand into the wall to give himself some room, but his bones would not straighten. He was trying to open his chest for air, but his trachea was crushed, and there was simply no way for him to breath.

She watched him wriggle. Chills ran through her

spine, and a smile began to develop over her face. He thrashed a little, and she watched with a wicked sense of satisfaction.

"So many things I could say to you, and I did rehearse the speech. I almost wish you could speak. I want to hear you tell me how you killed them, exactly what you did to her Jeep. What did you do to her? I have so many questions that have gone unanswered, you stupid fucking bastard."

Her angry voice trailed through clenched teeth. She wished she could stand up and pummel him to an unrecognizable ball of flesh that would take at least a hundred experts to pick up the pieces and learn his identity.

He tried to reach for her, "David, what do you need? Air? I know CPR," she said leaning closer, his face growing moist from her wet breath, "and I'll be damned to waste it on you." She released the hold of his hair and stood over him.

She could see his eyes zero in on her then roll slightly upward, just before disappearing into the back of his head. She collapsed the baton on the cement floor of the basement and shoved it into her pocket. She stepped over him and back to the top of the stairs.

She glanced back for a moment and then retrieved her bag. She carefully removed the brown Docker shoe and walked to the basement stairs. She placed it on the second step.

She made a quick mental inventory of her items, *purse, chalk, penlight, baton, fuzzy bear, purple ribbons, Ziploc bag, pool cue.*

"This ballerina bear, yes, I will leave you on David's bed, and the purple laces from the shoes, I will leave them in your home office, consider it a gift from me to you, asshole," she said in the darkness.

She had noticed a photograph of Rebecca and Hayley on the refrigerator, and she had planned on taking it but thought someone might notice. She swiped the picture and left the magnet, she placed it on the kitchen counter and laid the broken cue across it.

Wait, one more thing. The folder. She scooped up the folder and laid it open, revealing its contents. From her bag, she removed the text-chat conversation she had printed earlier and shoved it toward the back. She carefully placed the photo of Rebecca and Hayley in the center, and then replaced the broken cue.

Chapter 18

Allison rolled over and whispered to Terri, "Hey babe. I know it's early, but I have to get up soon."

Terri looked over at the LED display on the clock, 1:30 a.m. She blinked a couple of times, wondering if her eyes were blurry.

"It's 1:30 in the morning, where do you have to be at this hour?" She questioned. The sheets were still wrapped around their legs, holding them tied together.

"I need to be on a plane for New York," Allison told her bluntly.

"What? You didn't tell me you were going to New York," Terri was feeling more awake now.

Allison wisped the hair from Terri's eyes and caressed her cheek. Terri felt her fingers slide down her face from her temple to her neck, then across her chest.

"I have another assignment in New York. I have to leave this morning on the early flight," it seemed Allison was teasing, her voice was soft and fingers purposeful.

"You are kidding me, right?" Terri was drifting back to a soft sleep just listening to her talk. "When are you coming back?" She managed to murmur.

"I don't think I will be back at all, my dear," Allison said more clearly. Her fingertips traced Terri's face then back to her neck.

"What are you saying?" Terri was beginning to feel that sickening, not-so-comfortable butterfly feeling in the pit of her stomach. She turned to face Allison, pulling her hand down from her face, "What? You are leaving?"

"To be honest, I wasn't even sure if I would be here this long. It has been heavenly," she said with a smile. Allison began to stretch her legs out on the bed and uncover. Moving the pillow from beneath her head, she laid it on the floor and extended her arms above to the wall.

Terri was still confused as Allison began to sit up.

"Um, so that's it?" Terri was awake now. She watched as Allison picked the pillow up from the floor and used it as shield to cover her body while she walked to the bathroom. Dropping it just before she reached the door, Terri admired the strength in her back.

The sound of the shower sliced through the silence. Terri lay wondering how she felt about Allison leaving. *Then again, I still have Ryann*, she thought.

Terri got up and wandered to the bathroom; she turned the little night light on near the sink so Allison could see.

"What time does the plane leave? When do you have to be at the airport?" Terri was standing in the bathroom pondering her next move. She was emotional as she watched the steam conceal the mirror, not knowing if she had been used.

Terri couldn't resist peering behind the curtain, and she watched longingly as Allison washed her hair, the water streaming down her back. It seemed to fall off her buttocks to the shower basin in a smooth motion.

She steadied herself and lifted one foot in, needing now to be as warm as the water.

Allison turned as Terri enveloped her body in her arms. Kissing the wet from her neck, Terri asked, "just one more day?"

"No, no. I can't. And I really do have to be going. I still have to pick up my things at the hotel before I drive to the airport," Allison seemed a little distant, rinsing Terri's arms from her just as she had the soap. "Try to understand."

Allison turned the water off and stepped from the shower. She left Terri standing there in the cold atmosphere of the bath. She wrapped herself in a towel and returned to the bedroom.

Terri stepped out of the shower and patted enough of the water from her body so she wouldn't freeze and followed her. She stopped in the doorway and watched Allison dress quickly. She had already situated herself on the corner of the bed to put her socks on. She scooped up her jeans from the floor and had them zipped before Terri moved.

Terri wondered if the shock was keeping her from witnessing time as it unfolded. Allison looked around and picked up the last of her things, "I have to go. This has been wonderful, thank you."

Terri felt like whatever 'this' was, was vanishing right before her.

"I will call you, okay?" Allison asked as she started for the door.

Terri waited in the bedroom until she heard the house door close. The thunderous roar of the car starting broke her trance, and she went to the living room. She watched through the window, the taillights riding off in the distance.

She returned to the warmth of the bed and wrapped up. She lay there staring at the ceiling until she fell back asleep.

Chapter 19

Ring. Ring. Ring. Three rings in and Terri turned over to grab it, "Hello?" Her voice sounded as if she had been awake all night.

"Terri, it's Reese," he said quietly.

"Who?" Terri was still half asleep.

"Reese. Officer Reese. Do you think you can cover for Cooper?"

"David? What? Am I supposed to be at work? I thought we set the meeting for ten?" She was concerned she had missed her scheduled meeting.

"How long have I been sleeping?" She wrestled with the sheets again and was somehow entangled.

"No, no. It's only 8:00 a.m. you have a couple of hours, but Cooper said he would come in and help me with an interview this morning. He hasn't shown up, and I needed him here a half hour ago."

Reese had been preparing all morning for a breaking and entering suspect to come in. He thought he had his man and was finally going to have a crack at an interview.

"Cooper told me he would help guide me through from the listening room," Reese told her.

"Have you tried calling him?" Terri asked the obvious. She knew he wouldn't answer, especially if he had been entertaining the evening before. By that, she meant playing with the 'gaming club.' He had told her sometimes the online strategy games could take all night. She didn't understand it what his obsession was, but he had never missed work because of it before.

"Terri, my suspect is coming in and will be here in about a half hour. You know that case I was working from the north end, near the proposed new build?" Reese started to tell her about his investigation.

"Wait, what? Okay, give me a minute. I'm just

waking up. Let me call you back in a few minutes after I wash my face," it was an effort to buy some time, her head spinning.

"Terri, c'mon. I'll have coffee for you and a couple of donuts. Jack brought in bagels, and cream cheese and I will even toast it for you. Please," Reese was persistent; he needed her there.

"I'll be in, let me get dressed. Twenty minutes. And I'm not hungry right now, but coffee sounds good." Terri hung up the phone and spun her legs over the edge of the bed. She felt like a freight train struck her, but this time there was no alcohol involved. *Sleep deprivation, ugh.*

She grabbed a five-minute shower and threw on some clothes. She wore comfortable work jeans and a t-shirt. She grabbed a hooded sweatshirt on the way out the door. She would be in the back room watching and listening via surveillance monitors and microphones so dress clothes were not necessary. With the touch of a button on her headset, she could whisper in Reese's ear a question if he had forgotten to ask a question.

Terri called Cooper on the way to the office. His phone rang and went straight to voicemail. She sent him a few texts and asked him to contact her or Reese as soon as possible with no response. She thought about driving by his house, but she would have to drive by the office to get to it. *I better help Reese first. This wouldn't be the first time David didn't do something he promised to do,* she reasoned.

"Good morning, honey. When you wake, give me a call. I'm headed to the office this morning to give one of my partners a hand with an interview. Talk to you soon," Terri left a voice mail for Ryann.

She was already pulling into the parking lot of the police department when her phone rang back.

Shit. It's Ryann. Terri read the caller identification. "Hi, Hon," Terri decided to answer.

"Hi. I was so tired last night I didn't get a chance to call you back. It was such a nice morning for a run; I got up early and got a few miles in. I know you were a little upset last night, but do you want to meet since it is your day off?" Ryann asked her.

"Didn't you listen to my voicemail?" Terri asked.

"Uh, no. I just called you right back. I didn't want to miss you if you were headed outside. I know how you get busy doing something and one thing leads to the next, and I end up missing you completely!" The smile in Ryann's voice was evident. She sounded upbeat and rested as if she had been looking forward to spending the day with her.

"How about if I call you after work, I'm just pulling into the department," Terri started but was quickly interrupted.

"What? Work? You went to work?"

"Well, Reese called and said he needed me to help him today, and I have that meeting. It shouldn't take very long. We can do something after," Terri was hoping to spare some of the day.

"No. I don't think I will be waiting around for you to finish doing whatever you are doing today. You never put me first, how come Terri?" Ryann was pissed.

Terri wasn't sure how to respond or if she just thought Ryann was insensitive to her work demands. She held her breath for a second and then let Ryann have it, "Yes, work. I will be at work because I have something important to do."

"That's fine. I never thought I would be first on your list, but I sure as hell didn't want to be last. I'm making other plans, and for that matter, I have other plans for the rest of the week!" Ryann hung up as Terri began to speak.

"What in the..." there was nothing but the dial tone. *That stupid bitch hung up on me! Who the hell does she think she is?* Terri jammed the phone into her back pocket as she entered the police station. There was too much on her mind to let Ryann bother her now.

Terri and Reese finished the interview after obtaining a written confession from his suspect. His suspect was sitting in the back cell, handcuffed to the wall while Terri helped him complete his report.

"Thanks, Terri. I really appreciate it. We made really good time. You still have 45 minutes before your meeting."

"Reese, you'd better get him down to the County if you want to get him arraigned this afternoon," Terri reminded him the magistrate would not be available after 3 p.m. He still needed to have the prosecutor review and authorize the warrant before that could happen.

"I am finishing the warrant packet and request now, Terri. Thank you, again." He had a handful of reports and forms. He stuffed them in a folder, grabbed his suspect and headed for the County Jail.

Terri rewound the interview tapes and placed them in evidence for Reese. He might need them if the written confession wasn't enough for the prosecutor.

She sat down at her desk and turned the computer on. *45 minutes, I have to get some of these lab reports printed for the meeting,* she thought. She decided to check her emails before wading through the litany of information she wanted to go over. She was still waiting on the laboratory analysis from items collected at the Moore scene, and maybe that was waiting in her Email inbox.

"Junk, junk, bulletin, legal update, Forensic Lab-there you are," she was talking to herself in the office.

Terri read through the preliminary information on the stuffed bear, and the business card. No trace evidence, no prints. She read a little further before getting to the CODIS information, "DNA analysis," she stated.

Her eyes widened as she saw the name revealed from the blood analysis on the letter opener, Jeremy Michael Hines, "Holy shit."

Hitting print on the PDF, she closed the report, and a new email popped up, BancroftWCSD.gov. She quickly opened the Email and read it. "Officer Bradford, we received the print analysis on our stabbing victim, his name was Jeremy Hines. His registered address was 51172 Monica, so if you don't mind swinging by there to see if his family knows where he is or what happened to him. My personal number is 555-656-7654, give me a call when you read my Email."

She grabbed her phone to call Jones and Pierce. She would have to get a hold of Cooper and get the meeting started as soon as possible. She was hoping Cooper would have called her back by now. She checked her phone- *no messages*. She looked at the last call information, nothing since her call from Ryann. *I think I'll make some phone calls. Maybe Randy will bring me a donut, I should probably go grab something. It might be a long day.*

"Hey, Terri? You still here?" Jack called her from the front desk.

"Yes, sir. Do you want breakfast? I was thinking of heading over to Bob's for take-out," Terri asked him hoping he would say no. She wasn't in the mood to run all over town for Jack, not today.

"No, no. I brought in dinner from last night. Will you run over to Cooper's house? He isn't answering, and when I talked to him last night before he left, he said he would be in early to help Reese. I'm not even getting a text from him," Jack had some concern in his voice.

"Really? He is probably sleeping this one off," Terri remarked, assuming he had consumed a little over his limit while playing with his gamers.

"Please? I don't want to worry for the rest of the day? A personal favor, please? At least drive by and tell me if his car is in the driveway," Jack knew Terri would check on her partner so they both could rest easy on her day off.

"Yeah. I'll run by there on my way to grab food. He hasn't called me back either and we have a meeting shortly." Terri headed for the back door, "I'll have him call you, Jack," she yelled back as the door was closing.

Terri started out to the parking lot and gave Ryann a call. It went straight to voicemail. She wasn't going to leave a message. Instead, she called Trisha, "Trish? You working?" Terri said into the phone.

"Yeah, what are you up to? I thought you had a big meeting today?" Trisha asked, "Aren't you at work?"

"Yeah, I am. I came in early to help Reese..." Terri's sentence was cut off.

"You aren't working all day, though, are you? I thought you would have the rest of the day off?" Trisha was trying to act surprised.

"I did have the day off, except for my meeting. David didn't show up for an interview and Reese called me early to cover for him. Anyway, Ryann got pissed, and I haven't talked to her. I'm going to check on David and stop over to grab food before my meeting." Terri rushed the conversation as she neared David's house.

"Sure, okay. We'll talk about it when you get here. You are going to lose that girl, you know?" Trisha knew what she was talking about, but Terri really didn't care. There would be another one.

"I'm just about to David's. See you in a few minutes," Terri ignored her comment and pulled into the driveway. She sat in the car for a few minutes and called from her cell phone. *No answer. He should be up by now,* she thought.

"I'm in your driveway, call me back," Terri hung up and waited a few minutes. She got out of the car and walked to the garage. She twisted the handle and swung the outside entry door open. *Not locked.* There really had been no need in Waterford for locking doors and David would have felt no different.

His car was parked in the usual spot in the driveway. A tennis ball hung from the ceiling touching the windshield indicating he had pulled in far enough, and not too far.

She didn't pay much attention to it. *His car is here. Therefore he must be here*, she thought.

Terri turned her head and thought, *something is missing. What is not right in here?* She stood for a few moments looking around the garage; she saw his work car, the clean floor, meticulously placed tools, there was nothing cluttered or out of place. Somehow, that struck her as unusual.

She turned and started for the house. She called him one more time while she approached the door, then it occurred to her. *The garage was clean. How could David have been working on a car, when there is only his work car in the garage? And there are no tools? And the floor is clean?*

She called again. *There was still no answer.* Terri knocked loudly. It reminded her of the ritualistic police knock just before announcing a search warrant.

The glass in the door panes shivered from the heavy knock, "David?" She yelled into the closed door. Terri turned the knob; it was unlocked and she poked her head in.

She yelled a couple more times, "David! David?" She walked through the kitchen to the living room still calling his name, "David?" *Maybe he isn't home.* Terri thought he had probably stayed with someone, but it was unusual for him to miss work, and not answer his phone.

Before making her way to the bedrooms, she phoned him again. She could hear his phone ringing at a distance, and it took her to the basement stairs. "Oh My God!" Terri said out loud, almost dropping her phone.

She raced down the stairs to where David laid and checked for a pulse, "Oh, no. No, No, No!" She almost shrieked.

She stared at him in disbelief, his neck twisted to the side in an obviously distorted position. He was facing downward, half on his back and half on his side. It looked like his leg was broken and bent, the back of his head pressed against the wall, forcing him into a position of asphyxiation. He was obviously dead.

Chapter 20

    The entire Waterford Police Department and County Sheriff were at Cooper's house in a matter of 20 minutes. Terri phoned Captain Williams directly, then Jones. She blocked the driveway with her car before anyone arrived.

    "Terri, Oh My God...are you okay?" Jones was genuinely concerned. She was standing, leaning against her car waiting for someone, anyone to arrive. The look on her face was molded into complete shock.

    "I'm fine. I'm going back in to help," Terri turned and started back toward the house. She wanted to be as involved as possible; she couldn't believe it. Her partner, David Cooper was dead.

    "Maybe you shouldn't. Just wait until Pierce is done," Jones was not suggesting. He tried to grab her shoulder and stop her from getting into the house, but she quickly pulled away from him and was inside before he could catch up to her.

    Terri walked by Pierce as he stood in the kitchen. He had already taken pictures of the perimeter and was in the shooting more photographs from the view of the dining room. Jones stopped to talk to him for a few minutes, and then they both went after Terri.

    Jones stood with Terri as she stared down the stairs. "Come on, don't look," he said and turned her around.

    Pierce walked by them and continued down the stairs. He took seemingly endless photographs. He moved swiftly throughout the basement getting shots from every angle, and at least a hundred or more of the body.

    Normally it would only take forty or fifty photos to document the entire house, but Pierce was too stunned to notice he had already snapped so many.

"He tripped, Terri," Pierce managed to say. He had finished the basement photos. "It appears David tripped on the shoe he left on the stair. He broke his neck in the fall down and suffocated in positional asphyxia," Pierce could barely speak.

"Did you get the rest of the house?" Terri asked.

"No, I really don't see any reason we need any more than the area of the body. I took several overall shots; that should be good enough. What a shame." Pierce was visibly shaken. He exited the house and left Terri and Jones standing in the living room.

Terri walked through to the kitchen. She was dazed, not knowing what she was looking for. She thumbed through the items on the table; she found the photograph from the refrigerator, "Rebecca and Hayley," she said out loud.

Terri moved the short wooden stick that lay across the photo, "I just can't believe it."

She started to put the photo down when she realized what she was holding. *What is this?* She examined the short stick with a little more scrutiny. *This is a broken pool cue, the handle end.*

"Terri, come on. They are taking him out now," Jones grabbed her shoulder and held her arm, "Terri, come on."

She set the pool cue down where she had found it and went with Jones. He walked her out behind the gurney. They stood silently as they loaded Cooper into the hearse and they watched as it drove off.

"Randy, we have to go back in," Terri said.

"Let's get out of here, Terri. He is gone. I can't believe it either, but he is gone," he was trying to convince himself as much as he was trying to convince her.

"No, we will be going in- NOW!" Terri ordered him.

"Terri, it isn't going to help. Come on," Jones was trying to reason with her, knowing how upset she might be.

"You son of a bitch, we are going in," she told him through gritted teeth. She was trying not to arouse Pierce or the Captain or any other officer that might have still been on scene.

He had no choice but to follow her. She walked directly to the kitchen table and picked up the piece of pool cue and shoved it in his face.

"Do you recognize this?" She held it up for him to see.

"No. What? What are you talking about?"

"This. See this? Look at it. What is it?" Terri demanded he think about it.

"What does it look like? A pool stick?" She prompted him.

"Ok. A pool stick. So what?"

"Um, do you remember seeing this someplace else? Like Monica Street?" Terri was pushing his memory.

Holy fuck, Randy thought as the wheels started to turn. "The other half of the pool cue from the Moore murder? What? How?" Jones stammered, "It can't be. No, Terri. It isn't."

"I don't know, but it sure looks like it. Do you see a pool table anywhere around her? In his office? In his bedroom, in the basement?" She was forcing him to look at the obvious.

"I want to look through some of his other things. I mean, how does he have evidence from a crime scene he was never at?"

"Terri, stop. Do you know what you are saying?" Jones did not want to hear it.

He moved a couple of pieces of mail and knocked two on the floor in the process. His clumsiness uncovered a manila folder, "Game Stoppers, his video game club. He spent so much time with them," Jones remarked.

Jones was curious, and he opened the envelope to see what the infatuation with it was.

"Jesus, Terri. Team 2 Squared."

"What? What did you say?" She remembered the business cards found at the crime scenes.

"Team 2 Squared- it's the members of Cooper's club," Jones handed her several prefilled sheets.

"George Moore, Kevin Kramer, Jeremy Hines, Jason Winslow, Charles Anthony... these are prefilled sex offender verification sheets. These guys are all registered on Monica Street."

It was beginning to sink in now. "These guys were in Coop's 'gamer' club," Jones stated.

"Some club. David must have been registering them when he worked the desk during registration," Terri guessed.

"No wonder Moore came in on the last day. He was waiting for Cooper to come back from his vacation," Jones recalled how he had come in a day late to verify his address.

"Why would he kill them? What possible reason would he have to kill them?" Jones asked.

"Maybe he was making them pay. I mean, maybe he was charging a fee. Maybe they threatened to expose him. He had been taking a lot of vacations since Rebecca died. I don't know," Terri offered.

"I want to check out his home office. He has to have a computer area and a game console. He has to- it couldn't all be fake."

This was almost too difficult for Terri to understand. However, the clues kept adding up; David was a manipulative, conniving blackmailing bastard, selling his services to falsify sex offender addresses for a fee.

They entered the room together and immediately located a used square blue cue chalk upon the desk.

"Blue chalk," Terri said. She moved the keyboard, and the screen became active. It had been in sleep mode. A small child flashed on the screen, and Terri thought it might have been Hayley until the next young girl popped up. His screen savers were images of children. The color suddenly drained from her face as she found a stack of photographs beneath the keyboard. She was speechless.

"Terri? Terri!" Jones raised his voice snapping her out of the trance.

"You won't fucking believe this," Terri choked.

"What? What won't I believe?" Jones reached for the pictures, "What the fuck? Terri is this..."

Terri cut him off, "Child Porn," she finished his sentence. Terri looked around nervously, wondering if anyone else was in the room with them.

"Randy look at this," she picked up a printed-paper containing a chat-room conversation.

Jones took the paper and read it for himself, "Holy shit," he muttered, and then began to read it out loud:

"Ragin37: U there Sunni

Sunblock13: Yes

Ragin37: Whatcha doin

Sunblock13: TAY (thinking about you)

Ragin37: I was thinking about you too..." Jones stopped before reading anymore.

"Holy fuck, Terri...do you suppose that's how he lured them to that house?" Randy asked.

Terri didn't answer; she was listening and watching the screensavers.

He scanned the document then read a bit more from the bottom:

  "Ragin37: I would kiss you all over

Ragin37: what is your address

Sunblock13: 51172 Monica

Ragin37: U won't tell will you

Sunblock13: No. Y would I

Ragin37: I am older than U

Ragin37: Is there somewhere I can park where no one will see my car?

Sunblock13: the Meijer's down the street."

Terri, still in a state of shock over the photographs, "that's where we found Kramer and Hines' vehicles. In the parking lot."

She grabbed it from Jones's hands and returned it to the folder. She looked around for similar documents. Jones took the hint and continued his search as well. He began opening drawers and found another folder of documents. It is one thing to be a serial killer of pedophiles, but quite another to be a police officer who was also a pedophile.

She opened the top sliding drawer and saw an assortment of ribbons, pins, and pencils, and a letter opener, "Randy, look at this," she was holding the opener.

"It says 'CMT' on the handle. Randy, it says 'CMT'!"

"Jesus, Terri."

She located another folder in the side file door drawer, "APEX Industries, Insurance Specialties."

"Hey. Kramer and Moore worked for APEX, isn't this the same company? What else does it say?" Jones took the paper from her, "It's an insurance payout. It says it is for a payout of $500,000. "

"For who?" Terri asked, she continued looking through the desk.

"Rebecca and Hayley," Jones said flatly "Holy shit."

Her was heart racing as she found another folded set of documents in the second drawer. She opened them and read it to Randy, "These are divorce papers."

"What's in the other envelope, Terri?" Jones asked.

There was an envelope taped to the inside cover of the folder. She opened it carefully and started to read:

"David, you are a monster. I want a divorce immediately. I want full custody of Hayley, and you will stay out of our lives forever. If you don't, I will go to the police, and you will pay for what you have done. You will not do to our daughter what you did to me. She is too young. You took me from my sister and my family. My mother and father are dead now and I have only Hayley and my sister. Please, leave us alone."

"Do you think he killed them too?" Jones said it as if he already believed it.

"I don't know. I didn't know him at all. It is beginning to look like he did kill them," Terri saw a scandal headed for the front page.

"Randy, you will say nothing about this. Gather these items up and put them in my trunk. We will talk about this later. Or maybe we will never talk about this. How dare David Cooper disgrace our police agency?" Terri was stern, offended, and mad. Her head spinning at the thought of her stellar reputation as a police officer marred by one incident.

"Terri, we have to solve the murders of Moore and Kramer. Does it seem to you David killed them?"

"How could he have *not* killed them?" Terri demanded he think about it. She replayed the evidence in her mind; even if it were circumstantial, the evidence they had already found was enough for her.

"Randy, there is the broken cue, the chalk, the screensavers, what else do we need for you to understand? We even have the insurance policy, Kramer and Moore both working for APEX, the gamer club, and the business cards." Terri had laid it out in two sentences.

Randy dutifully gathered as much as he could. They collected the items from the home office and went to the bedroom to search for more evidence.

"Nothing out of the ordinary in here," Jones said. "Except that purple ballerina bear and those purple ribbons on the bed," Terri pointed, she was pissed. Every element was adding up to a conviction.

Jones was going through his drawers. He found a significant amount of cash stuffed into a sock, "Perfect hiding place. Terri, isn't this where we tell people not to stash their cash?" He found some humor and his police joked eased some tension.

"Is there anything else?" She ignored the humor.

"Yes. A notebook and an address book, and a few more pictures," Jones pulled the items out and tossed them on the bed.

"Let me see. What's this?" Terri opened the address book and found the pictures of the underage females. They were listed alphabetically with full physical descriptions, emails, and phone numbers.

"Jesus, he was a very sick man," Terri also observed sex offender names listed at the bottom of each page.

"He was running an offender ring. Selling information, training offenders, covering for them and their escapades. He provided a house for them he knew no one would question," Terri sat on the bed, deflated.

"Is that it, Randy? I can't look at anymore," she asked him.

"Let me pick up the shoe Terri, we should collect it," Jones told her as they busied themselves collecting the evidence that would convict him – and the Waterford Police Department.

"Terri, we can't let the Moore and Kramer murder go unsolved," he said again.

"They won't Randy; we will talk to the prosecutor and explain it. Maybe we will disclose it to the Captain, and she can make this go away. There is no investigation left to do," she explained.

Still outside, Captain Williams ordered everyone back to the department for debriefing. The medical examiner finished her on-scene responsibility and left the funeral home director in charge of transporting the body to the morgue division of the hospital. There would be an autopsy as a matter of protocol and then his body would be transferred to the funeral home in town.

Chapter 21

Terri tried to call Ryann on the way back to the department. *No answer.* She didn't want to leave a voicemail; she wasn't sure what she would say anyway. She suddenly felt alone and anxious, but she needed to talk to somebody.

"Hello?" Trisha answered the phone.

"Trish, David's dead," her words were choked and emotional. Silence fell between the two of them.

"What?" Trisha said in disbelief; she was almost in tears empathizing with the pain her best friend must have felt.

A moment passed before Terri could speak again, "He's dead. Fell down his stairs and broke his neck." Terri's voice trembled, "I am on my way back to the department, and I will call you later."

"What?" Trisha said again, "What can I do?"

"Nothing. I don't know. I will call you, okay?"

Terri wasn't sure what she wanted to say, but it felt better having told someone about David's death.

"I called Ryann but she didn't answer. That's just as well because she is already out of town."

"What? Ryann is gone? Oh, Terri. I'm sorry. David is dead? Ryann is gone? I'm coming over," Trisha told her.

Terri did not object, she needed her friend now more than ever before.

The next 24 hours were a blur. The funeral was an enormous ordeal for such a small town. The entire community supported the fallen officer. Police agencies from around the state sent pairs of officers, and they filled the tiny funeral home and spilled out onto the street.

There were police cruisers lined up along every

road for two miles. There was an impressive 36-vehicle motorcade and 24 motorcycles. A team of horseback officers followed along with streams of patrol units with their lights activated. Agencies from across the nation were represented either by patrol unit or staff.

Officer David Cooper was treated with dignity, respect, and had an honorable traditional police funeral. "I think I am going to be sick," Terri mentioned to Jones.

"You, I was a pallbearer, Terri. I'm sickened. I've carried soldiers that deserved more, that risked more, that gave their lives honorably, and I was forced to carry Officer Cooper," Jones was completely stoic.

Chapter 22

It was the day after the funeral and Terri was trying to pull herself together, she was still shocked at what she and Jones had uncovered.

"Terri, do you want me to ride with you to Havelock?" Jones had asked her.

She was sitting in her office staring at the scene investigation report and the photographs that were taken at Cooper's house. She was genuinely depressed and confused.

"I don't know. No, not yet. I still can't believe it," Terri was shocked.

"I don't know what the right thing to do is, Randy. David was a murderer. He was a pedophile," she leaned back in her chair.

"How did we not know? How did *I* not know?" Terri stared disbelievingly.

"He's dead now, Terri. There is no point in getting worked up over it. At least not now," Jones didn't know how to offer his support. They were both traumatized.

"Those photos. Those chats. Do you think he really killed all three of those guys?" Terri was serious.

"I don't know. It looks like it, doesn't it?" Jones sat down on the desk, nearly knocking over Terri's Diet Coke.

"I went to the Meijer today and recovered two vehicles," Jones told her, he was tying up loose ends.

"You did?" Terri paused to listen.

"Yes. A Ford registered to Kramer, and a Dodge that was registered to Hines," he told her.

"Is that a fact?" Terri asked. She would believe almost anything he said to her.

"Yes, they were both parked in the same area. Those were the same parking spaces described in the online-chats between Coop and them. He set them up. He was the one that told them to park there," Jones told her.

"Did you search them?" Terri asked if an inventory search of the vehicles had been completed.

"Yes, and we found directions. They were directions to 51172 Monica. Kramer had left them in his vehicle; he must have memorized the numbers. I believe you are right. I think he was killed on Monica Street at the same address as Moore," Jones told her.

"We need proof that he also killed Hines. We need something."

"There is something else. I can't quite put my finger on," she looked at Jones.

"I keep going over these photos and David's autopsy. His cause of death was a broken neck leading to asphyxia," she said.

"Yes, just like the other murder victims, how ironic," Jones commented without remorse. "He probably got what he deserved," he couldn't believe he just said that to Terri.

"I'm sorry, Terri," he apologized.

"It seems so surreal," she began to examine the photographs, one by one.

"I never knew David played pool," Terri commented about the used blue chalk on the edge of his computer keyboard, "It doesn't look like he was home much at all, considering the dust."

She felt as though she never really knew him, outside of work, anyway. Even who he pretended to be at work was questionable.

"Maybe it was a souvenir, Terri. You know, just one more memoir of his accomplishments to shelf along with his trophies and awards," Jones offered.

"I just feel like I need more proof. Proof that he killed Kramer, other than the blue chalk on his face," Terri commented. "I can accept he killed Moore, after all, we found the other half of the pool cue that was used to kill him," Terri said.

"You mean, other than the 2 Squared? That club Jessica already told us he was a part of? Oh, and the crushed larynx and the splinters of wood?" Jones lacked sympathy.

"Yes, just one more piece. I need one more piece; I'm not ready to accept this," Terri told him.

Suddenly, she snapped straight up in her chair. She was staring at a photograph of Cooper's twisted body along the stairwell, "Randy...is that what I think it is? Look."

Terri pointed at the stair step near the top, "Do we have these photos on disc? Did Mike download his photos yet? I mean, uh, can we look at these on the computer?"

"Yeah, they are on disc. I have it here, let's take a look." Jones shuffled some envelopes and files on Pierce's desk and found one not labeled, but sitting on top of a folder marked, 'The Coop'.

"Well, I think this is the one," he handed it to Terri, and she inserted it into the drive.

The auto-play program accepted the disc and a box indicating nearly two hundred photos popped up. The icons became images as they began to load.

"Yeah, this looks like one of them," Terri quickly opened the photo viewer and went to the one of Cooper lying on the stairs. She zeroed in on the steps above him and zoomed to 400% magnification, "Holy Shit."

"What? It looks like he tripped on the shoe and fell down the stairs," Jones replied.

"What are you looking for?" He said again as he looked at the photo details. He was trying to see what Terri saw.

"Yes, yes. See this?" Terri was standing, her finger pressed into the monitor screen, "Print this Randy, just like it is. I just want this part of the picture."

Terri pushed her desk chair out of the way and reached for the binder marked 'Kramer.' She flipped to the tab marked, 'photographs'.

"Randy, look. See this? This is a men's size ten

brown Dockers shoe. See the photograph of the bottom?" Terri outlined the shoe tread and pointed at the markings.

"Now look. See this shoe on David's stair? This is just the bottom, but it has the same markings, and it is labeled 'Dockers' with the emblem beneath the word. See this number, it's a '10' isn't it?"

"What are you saying, Terri? You think Coop didn't trip on his own shoe? That it may be more than a coincident that maybe those guys wore the same shoes, or at least the same size and style?" Jones was comparing the shoes and drawing the same conclusions.

"What size shoe did Cooper wear?" Jones asked.

"Just because I'm his partner doesn't mean I know what his boot size was. And I sure as fuck didn't know he was into little girls!" She was pissed.

"What did you guys do with the contents of his locker?" Terri knew they might have already discarded his things.

"The lock is still on it. We haven't touched it. His issued weapons were at his house, so we really didn't need to go through it." Jones and Terri stared at each other. They nearly tripped over one another getting to the locker room.

"Are those bolt cutters still in the garage?" Terri's asking sounded more like an order for him to retrieve them.

He was back in minutes, and they quickly cut the lock from his locker. Uniform shirts were hung with the plastic wrap from the dry cleaner. He had a shaving kit resting on the top shelf, his gym bag hanging from the back hook. On the bottom of his locker was a pair of military-style police boots.

Jones grabbed them and immediately flipped the bottoms up to the palm of his hand – "12".

"Twelve?" Terri asked.

"Twelve," he repeated, "That spineless bitch excuse for a cop murdered Hines, too."

Chapter 23

It had been two days after the funeral, and the town was still stunned by the loss. Waterford Police Department had never lost an officer in the line of duty, nor had they ever lost one that didn't pass from natural causes; the sting was still fresh.

They sat huddled around the open flames of the night fire and were a few beers in. Terri had invited Jones and Pierce over to hash out some of the details of the last few weeks. They were exchanging thoughts and assumptions; they were trying to make sense of it all.

Jones started, "He seriously tripped and fell down the damn steps."

"Broke his God damned neck," Pierce finished his sentence. Pierce had slammed his first two and appeared to be taking the death of his fellow officer very hard.

"Broke his neck in a few places, suffocated himself. I mean he fell with his head against that wall, broke his arm. How could he turn himself to breathe?" Randy explained.

"He was a sex offender, a pedophile, Mike," Terri found herself saying. She was staring at the fire, drinking her beer and had not heard what Randy and Mike were talking about.

"What? What did you just say, Terri?" Pierce was suddenly attentive.

"A pedophile, he was the fourth one. He was the fourth pawn in the game. The two squared kingpin. It was Officer David Cooper," her speech was a little slurred.

"What? What the fuck are you are saying, Terri?" He found himself fiercely protective of his fellow brother in blue.

"Mike, listen. We have the evidence. We have

the proof. Tell him, Randy," she deferred in her slightly intoxicated state.

"She's right Mike," Jones felt close enough to call him Mike, "we have the proof."

"Jarhead, you better not be fucking with me, or you are going to find out how a real Marine fights. You puke, are you telling me a fellow brother was a God damn pedophile?" Pierce was suddenly sober.

"Mike, yes. He was, and I have to believe he killed his wife and daughter, and also Moore, Kramer, and Hines," Jones slammed the last of his beer and motioned to Terri for another from the fireside cooler.

"You better God damn explain yourself Jarhead," Pierce was pissed, the fire in his eyes brighter than the small outside fire itself.

"Okay, give me a minute to explain," he waited for Terri to hand him another beer.

"I want facts and evidence," Pierce demanded.

Terri opened the bottle before handing Jones the beer. She chucked the metal cap into the fire.

"I brought some Crown for shots, now is a good time to get one done," Jones reached for a paper sack he had nestled beneath his chair. He ripped the seal and passed the bottle around. He passed it around the fire.

"Give it to me, Jarhead, and it better damn well be good," Pierce was pissed. He took a slug from the bottle and expected Jones to provide him with the evidence.

"Okay, Mike. I think it is best to show you what we found at Coop's place," Terri knew he would need hard evidence to be convinced.

"Let me show him the photos we took, Randy. Then he can look at them while you explain," Terri pulled out her cell phone and clicked the photos icon. She handed her phone to Randy so he could show Pierce.

"Okay, the first photos are of Coop's place. We are going to start backward, so you understand how all of this took place," Jones started to explain when Terri interrupted.

"Mike, you have to start with the premise that David was wrong, he is a suspect in this matter. David is the one we have been looking for the whole time," she was sincere. "You know he was never around when these murders took place, and he always had some excuse for not being at work, remember?"

"Your point being?" Pierce was still upset as he took another shot and handed the bottle back to Jones.

"I don't even know where to start, except with the death of Coop's wife and kid. You know when they were killed last year on the curve at Stern Creek?" Jones asked.

"Everybody knows that Jarhead, go on," Pierce continued to drink, he had no patience.

"Well, it looks like there could not have been a fire or explosion like Coop said in his report," Jones explained.

"What the fuck are you talking about, Jarhead?" Pierce asked. "We saw it, we all saw it."

"For starters, you know that Rebecca knew that curve. Everybody that lives in Waterford knows that curve. Why in the hell would she be traveling so damn fast around that curve? Think about it for a second. You can't take that curve faster than 25, and everyone knows it. Why did Coop's report say she took it at 75 mph?" Jones offered a question meant to make Pierce think.

"And the gas line. Coop told everyone she was alive. He told us that he had spoken with her, and we all saw the fiery mess of the vehicle afterward. It was horrible, remember, Mike?" He asked him to remember that fateful day.

"Coop told us she struck a gas line and the car started on fire, she was trapped and couldn't get out. He couldn't even get his daughter out of the car, remember Mike," Jones wanted him to remember.

Pierce sat there drinking, staring blankly into the fire. "We saw it, we all saw it," Pierce commented, not looking up.

"Remember how we all said we would have

scorched ourselves trying to get our children out, no matter the cost. Remember that Mike?" Jones was pushing him.

Pierce recalled the scene had been horrific and the bodies badly burned.

"Think about this Mike, was an autopsy done?" He asked him.

Jones did not wait for his reply, "No, Mike. An autopsy was not done. The bodies were badly burned, and because David was a cop, a friend, a confidant, we believed him."

"They were dead on impact," Terri chimed in.

"What's your fucking point?" Pierce was unwilling to believe what they were eluding to.

"The point is, Mike, there are no gas lines on the curve on the Stern Creek bend," Jones told him.

"What?" His forehead crinkled in a question.

Terri decided it was her time to speak, "That's the truth, and it is a flood zone, Mike. There are no gas pipelines, only water lines, and water drains."

"What?" He could not comprehend what they were telling him.

"Mike, there are no gas lines in the area. Therefore, Rebecca did not strike a gas line," Terri told him straight out.

"But the fire? The vehicle was engulfed. You were there Terri. You saw it for yourself," Pierce reminded her she was an eyewitness to the event.

"Yes, I believed David. He told me there was a gas line. He is the one that did the investigation remember? He told me the fire was too hot to approach. He wouldn't let me try, he held me back. Mike, they may have already been dead," Terri told him. She really didn't know, but looking back, and with the information that she had now, that was probably the most likely scenario.

"How the fuck do you know?" Pierce questioned, the alcohol getting to his head.

"Because I do. I was investigating the scene with an insurance company, and I saw water line markers. I looked for other markers, but they were all water line markers and drain markers. You know that road floods on that turn because of Stern Creek. He had us fooled; he had us believing there were gas lines, but how could there be?" Terri was rambling; she was unfolding the information for herself as well as Pierce. The alcohol loosened her mind enough to enable her to view the incident through a different set of lenses.

"Then there is the insurance policy, Mike," Jones grabbed the folder and flipped to the first page. He handed it to Pierce.

"See, there was an insurance policy for Rebecca and Hayley," Jones pointed to the amount.

"Half a million dollars?" Pierce said incredulously.

"Yes, but that's not it. Look at the name of the insurance company, Mike. Look at the name of the agency," Jones prompted him to read further.

It seemed a full five minutes before Pierce was able to say anything, "APEX Insurance."

"Yes, APEX, that is the insurance company Hines worked for," Jones stated.

"And Moore did also. David probably saw that they were both sex offenders and contacted them," Terri commented.

"You are full of shit," Pierce said.

"Well, we found this insurance policy authored by Hines in David's desk. Look at the amount, and look when it was dated," Jones showed him the next photo on Terri's phone.

"Where did you guys get this information? Where was this photo taken and when?" Pierce demanded.

"We found it when we were looking through David's things at his house. You were there, too. You were taking photographs. Jones and I were looking through his things," Terri explained.

"So you found a receipt?" Pierce continued to drink.

"Not just a receipt, an insurance receipt for half a million made payable to Coop upon the death of Rebecca and Hayley," Jones explained the insurance claim and canceled check.

"Coop got half a million when they died?" Pierce asked.

"He did. He got half a million," Jones told him.

All three sat silent for a few moments drinking their beers.

"Another round?" Terri asked. She was already reaching into the cooler. She tried to break the mounting tension.

"Now look at the next picture, Mike. It is on the computer keyboard in Coop's office. You see that, what is that?" Jones asked.

"It's, well, it's pool cue chalk," Pierce remarked.

"Yes, it's pool cue chalk. The same pool cue chalk that was smudged on Kramer's face, and the same pool cue chalk we found on Moore's neck. It is the same pool cue chalk we found on Monica Street," Jones told him.

"No, it can't be," Pierce was in denial.

"What about this stick?" Jones showed him another picture of the evidence collected at Cooper's home.

"What the fuck is this?" Pierce demanded.

"Half a pool cue. Notice it is splintered on the end? This could have been the murder weapon," Jones told him.

"Could have been! This is not evidence you puke, show me the evidence!" Pierce demanded.

"Mike, hold on. You are getting worked up, and you haven't even heard the whole story. Relax yourself; he is trying to show you the busted end of a pool stick. Do we really have to send it to the lab so they can match the splinters and the ends up to the same piece of wood?" Terri asked.

"Do you really want us to let the public know this was David all along?" She asked him.

"And look, look at this, too. The shoe. The shoe was a size 10. The shoe on the steps was a size 10,"

Jones jumped around a bit, he was uneasy in his chair.

"Mike, look at it. Randy and I looked at David's shoes. His shoes were a size 12. Why would he have a size 10 on the stairs? We figured he kept it as a souvenir," Terri interjected.

"A souvenir?" Pierce questioned.

"Yeah, there was only one shoe with Kramer in the box. Remember, his shoe was size 10. Why would David have size 10 shoes at his house unless he kept it from Kramer? I bet if we compared the two shoes, one would be the right and the other the left," Terri challenged him to test her.

"What if you are right? So what? He had one shoe that was size 10. Maybe he bought the wrong size shoe?" Pierce defended him.

Terri reached back into the cooler to help herself, it was her fourth one, and she was feeling no pain.

"Did you find the other shoe?" Pierce asked.

She handed another beer to Jones, and he quickly drank a third of it before continuing.

Pierce did not wait for the response, "A fucking shoe. That's all you got? You've got an ill-sized shoe that he happened to have on his steps? It's going to take more than a God damn shoe."

"We found these, too," Jones handed him an envelope.

"What the fuck is this?" Pierce said as he threw them down at his feet, "I want to hear the evidence, tell me what you think you have. What evidence could you possibly have against a fellow cop that could convince me?" He demanded.

"David was a part of a gamer club, yes?" Terri questioned him.

"Everybody knew that. Some Dragon's Slayer something, why? What does that have to do with murder?"

"We found out the Dragon's Slayer Club was 2 Squared," Jones told him.

"2 Squared? What the fuck is that?" Pierce was

not entertained. In fact, Pierce's face was red and his neck swollen from his increased blood pressure.

"2 Squared. It was a group of four child molesters who were communicating online in a group club. They were learning how to court young girls for sex," Jones was serious.

"Wait, what? How the fuck do you know that?"

Pierce reached toward the cooler for another beer. He could not believe his ears and he did not know what else to do but to keep drinking.

"Damn it, Mike. David sat at the desk the first week of sex offender registration, right? He registered these assholes to the address on Monica to keep them secret. They were part of his Dragon Club, which wasn't the dragons at all, it was 2 Squared, and there were 4 of them," Terri blurted, she could not understand how Pierce did not see it.

"Jesus, Terri, I'm getting to that," Jones gulped his beer. "Shots, everyone?" He asked again passing the bottle.

"Okay, so 2 Squared. I remember that from a business card, what does that have to do with the price of tea in China?" Pierce was buzzed and defensive.

"2 Squared was on the business cards. And it was in Coop's folder. He was the mastermind behind the 2 Squared group," Jones told him. He pointed to the folder Pierce had thrown at his feet.

"2 Squared was the gamer club?"

"Yes, these guys met online, shared information, tips, techniques, and ideas for convincing young girls to meet with them," Terri explained.

"Why would he kill them? Why would Coop kill his wife and only child? I do not understand your leap. It seems to me you guys are fishing," Pierce was ready for another shot.

"Jarhead, do you believe this shit? You believe Coop registered these guys on Monica Street to cover for them?" Pierce asked.

"I think he was the one working the desk during

the first week of the registration period. I believe I was working when these guys came in and wanted to know where he was. I believe he was off when these guys were killed if that is what you are asking," Jones was honest.

"Let's say that is true. Why would he kill these guys? What possible motive would he have for killing these guys?" Pierce was demanding an answer.

"Mike, calm the fuck down, here," Terri leaned forward and picked up the folder. She handed it back to Pierce. "You need to shut the fuck up and listen. Trust me. Randy and I are not happy with what we are telling you, but it all adds up and it is the truth."

"Get on with it, what else do you have?" Pierce needed more, "Bring on the facts, Jarhead. The facts. Who are you Jarhead? And just who the fuck do you think you are to throw another brother under the bus? Give me the God damn facts."

"Mike, calm the fuck down," Terri threw another log on the fire and sat back in her chair. "Randy and I would not be coming to you with this information if we didn't think it was true. Stop being an asshole and shut up and listen."

"Kramer, Moore, and Hines. All three were killed with a blunt strike to the throat, right?" Jones asked Pierce.

"Okay," he agreed.

"All three were sex offenders, agreed?"

"Okay," Pierce agreed again.

"All three were registered to 51172 Monica Street, is that true?" Jones asked.

"Go on," Pierce was listening, gripping his beer and watching the fire.

"All three of them belonged to an online group called '2 Squared'," Jones stated.

"How do you know that?" Pierce questioned.

"I told you we found the folder that explained what 2 Squared was with a group of names at Coop's house. Jessica also told me the group existed when I gave her that name from the back of the business card. Remember? It was written on the back of the business card we found in Moore's wallet?" Jones explained it again.

Pierce nodded his head in acknowledgement that he remembered.

"We found a folder of names at Coop's house. It had the name 2 Squared on it, and it listed Moore's name and others. There were online chat room conversations with Moore and Kramer. We also found one for Hines. Isn't that right Terri?" He asked her.

"That's true. It looks like David was the mastermind behind the online chats with underage girls," Terri explained. "You have the folder on your lap."

"Okay, it doesn't explain why you think he killed them," Pierce was still not convinced.

"Maybe they knew what he was up to, that he was into children," Terri said. "Maybe they had been paying him to register them during the first part of the month, and when he didn't do it, they threatened to expose him," Terri guessed.

"They were part of the club, then found out he was a police officer after the fact and threatened to expose him." Jones offered.

"We don't know, Mike. But he had these chats, and the evidence, and the motive," Terri explained. She pointed to the folder Pierce was holding.

"I'm not sure we want to go public with a pedophile police officer," she did not want to trash the Waterford Police Department.

"I don't know. What else do you have?" Pierce wanted another drink. He was a true military man and believed the enemy was the enemy and it was inconceivable to him that a member of the 'team' could be the enemy.

"Don't you think it is odd that Cooper just happened to be out of town when these murders happened? Those Waterford PD cards with Coop's name on them, do you still think that is some kind of coincidence?"

"Besides the pictures, shoe, pool cue, chalk smudge, and his initials on the registry forms at the beginning of each month, we have no other proof. I mean, I guess we could do a search warrant for his computer. Do we really want to go that far? Do we really need to expose one of our own now that he is dead?" Terri asked both of them.

Pierce thought for a moment, then he asked, "Okay, say you two are right. David offed these guys. He tripped on his souvenir shoe. Now what?"

They sat in silence before Terri spoke again, "I don't know Mike. How come you didn't know? Or did you? Maybe you knew and you were covering up for him. Maybe you were like every other cop covering up for him."

Pierce stood up as if to confront her physically. Jones stood as well and they met face to face. "Sit down, Mike," he instructed in a fierce military tone.

"Where were you when he was online soliciting minors for sex? Why did you let him use his work computer to look at child porn? Isn't his work space next to yours?" Terri was driving home a point.

"Do you want forensic analysis of the evidence, or do we want two unsolved homicides of pedophiles?" Terri asked him.

"Do you want us all to go down because of that sick-fuck? The Captain? Me? You? Jones? Because of what one officer did? You know the public will blame us for supporting him, they will call for our heads. They will believe we were all in on it. They will think it was a mass conspiracy to cover for him. Is that what we want?"

"No, no. I don't think so," Jones stated.

"Do you want your credibility, your reputation destroyed with a single statement? You, oh great Detective Pierce, had a child molesting serial killer sitting next to you and you didn't know?" Terri was genuinely concerned about the career she had built over the last 20 years. A career of integrity, honesty, and courteous.

"I have to agree with Jarhead, no. No, I don't think so," Pierce agreed.

They sat in silence for a few moments. Each one reflecting upon the cost of revealing the truth. Weighing the professional cost of reputation and possible future employment.

Pierce shifted uncomfortably in his chair before leaning toward Jones, "Shots?"

"Of course," Jones leaned down to pick up the near-empty bottle as Pierce stood up.

He flipped to folder open and saw photographs of very young females, children. He saw the insurance forms, the cancelled checks, the list of names, and the online chats.

The world stood still as the crackling of the fire seemed to be mocking them. Slowly, Pierce fed the folder of evidence into the fire. They did not exchange conversation, none of them wanting to admit they didn't see this one coming.

Chapter 24

The phone in Allison's pocket gave one short burst for the incoming message. It was a single word programmed to flash a notification for the text – "Good."

"Hi, honey, where are you?" Allison called her best friend. "I just received your one button press text that you are good. I'm guessing you are on the ground now?" Allison referred to the locket Ryan wore dutifully around her neck.

"I'm on my way, the plane just hit the runway, and we are coasting to the gate. I have luggage, and I have to pick that up at the carousel. I will be downstairs in a 30," Ryann told her.

"I am already here. I am parked near the shuttle bus stop," Allison remarked.

Ryann had two suitcases when she exited the airport. She stood on the sidewalk waiting for Allison to drive by. Not seeing her right away, she walked through the car rental parking and bus shuttle. She spotted her in a black BMW; she was waiting ahead of the transport buses.

"Hi, Rye," she said and loaded her suitcases into the trunk.

"It's over. It is all over now," Allison told her as they embraced. The hug was longer than a typical hug, their arms wrapped around each other completely. There was a sense of relief between the two of them.

Ryann cried as they held hands on the drive to her mother's home. Once they arrived, Allison was the first to get out. She popped the trunk and grabbed the luggage; together they walked to the home of Mrs. Kisne.

"Mom, I'm home," Ryann said into the doorbell speaker.

She heard the buzz of the unlocking mechanism and pushed the door open.

"Mom?" Ryann called into the corridor.

"Ryann Christine! My baby girl, I am so glad you are home, I am so proud of you, thank you. Please, please, both of you come in. Allison's sister is already here; she arrived yesterday."

"Jess! I am so glad you made it home, I have been worried about you," Allison told her as they hugged in the hall.

"I would do anything for my sister; you know that," Jessica told her.

"I am not sure what to say, I feel like justice has been finally served," Mrs. Kisne told her.

"Mrs. Kisne, I love Ryann like she was my own sister, as much as Jess. I loved Rebecca too, and I'm so sorry I didn't get to meet Hayley," Allison said.

They walked into the living room where Mrs. Kisne had prepared a cheese plate and wine was chilled.

"You would have loved them; I would give almost anything to have my daughter and my granddaughter back. But I know that cannot be," Mrs. Kisne said.

"I know mom. We can't go back, but we can move forward from here knowing he is dead. He will never hurt another child, and he will never coach another pedophile," Ryann's eyes welled up as she fought back the tears.

"A toast everyone," they raised their glasses at Mrs. Kisne's proposal, "to CMET."

The clang of glasses sounded with the celebration drink to the Child Molester Eradication Team.

Made in the USA
Monee, IL
16 December 2021